WORKBOOK TO ACCOMPANY

Music

IN THEORY AND PRACTICE

VOLUME I

Ninth Edition

Bruce Benward
Late of the University of Wisconsin–Madison

Marilyn Saker
Eastern Michigan University

Mc
Graw
Hill
Education

WORKBOOK TO ACCOMPANY MUSIC IN THEORY AND PRACTICE, VOLUME I, NINTH EDITION

Published by McGraw-Hill Education, 2 Penn Plaza, New York, NY 10121. Copyright © 2015 by McGraw-Hill Education. All rights reserved. Printed in the United States of America. No part of this publication may be reproduced or distributed in any form or by any means, or stored in a database or retrieval system, without the prior written consent of McGraw-Hill Education, including, but not limited to, in any network or other electronic storage or transmission, or broadcast for distance learning.

Some ancillaries, including electronic and print components, may not be available to customers outside the United States.

This book is printed on acid-free paper.

5 6 7 8 9 10 QVS/QVS 21 20 19 18 17

ISBN 978-0-07-749331-8
MHID 0-07-749331-1

Contents

Preface

The workbooks to accompany *Music in Theory and Practice,* volumes 1 and 2, provide assignments to augment, in depth and breadth, those printed in the texts. The chapters of the workbooks bear the same titles as those of the texts and are directly correlated with them. The compositions in the anthology sections are referred to in the assignments, but the instructor is free to use these pieces in any way he or she feels is appropriate.

The workbooks contain three different types of assignments:

1. *Drill.* This type of assignment acquaints students with the material in the corresponding chapters of the text. Learning to spell chords in various keys, distinguishing between chords in isolation, and identifying musical designs in artificially prepared situations are examples of drill exercises.

2. *Analysis.* This type of assignment acquaints students with music literature, permits them to view chapter material in its actual setting, and allows them to observe conformity to as well as digression from the norm. These exercises will also improve sight-reading ability and dexterity in analysis.

3. *Composition.* After the extensive drill and comprehensive analysis assignments, students are encouraged to try employing musical ideas, chord progressions, phrase relationships, and so on in their own musical compositions. If the devices that were drilled and analyzed can be successfully manipulated in a composition, one of the most important goals in the study of music theory will have been achieved.

The workbooks include guided review and self-testing sections. Each chapter contains a suggested strategy for reviewing and learning the material. Students often find that the study skills they have developed for other courses do not work well in learning music theory. The guided review sections present a step-by-step process involving reading, playing musical examples, and writing, which will help ensure success in learning the material.

Each chapter concludes with a sample chapter test covering the essential concepts of the chapter. Answers for all chapter tests are contained in a section beginning on page 235. These tests allow the student to identify areas of strength and weakness before in-class examinations.

Resources available from the McGraw-Hill Online Learning Center for this workbook include assignment templates compatible with Finale® music notation software and recordings for a majority of the compositions included in the anthology (recordings are identified with the following graphic: ♫). For instructors, a printable version of the corresponding *Workbook Solutions Manual* is available in addition to supplemental drill and testing materials. Visit www.mhhe.com/mtp9 for these items.

CHAPTER 1
Notation

A. Rewrite this melody using the clef provided. Also add proper meter and key signatures.

Saint-Saëns: Septet in E-flat Major, op. 65.

1.

2.

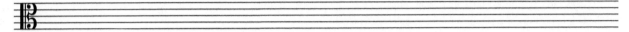

3.

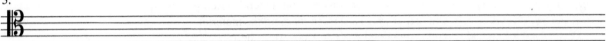

4.

B. Write the letter name for each tone and indicate the octave identification.

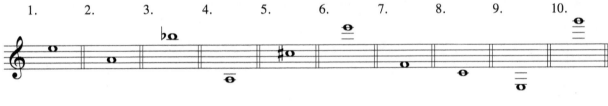

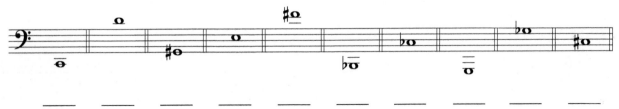

C. Write the letter name for each tone and indicate the octave identification.

1.   2.   3.   4.   5.   6.   7.   8.   9.   10.

___   ___   ___   ___   ___   ___   ___   ___   ___   ___

D. Lower each pitch one half step by either adding or deleting an accidental. Do not change the letter name of the tone.

1.   2.   3.   4.   5.   6.   7.   8.   9.   10.

Write your answers here:

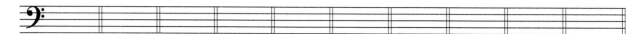

E. Raise each pitch one half step by either adding or deleting an accidental. Do not change the letter name of the tone.

1.   2.   3.   4.   5.   6.   7.   8.   9.   10.

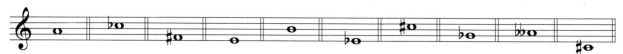

Write your answers here:

F. Rewrite this melody using the values expressed by the new meter signatures.

1.

2.

3.

G. Rewrite each phrase, correcting the errors in notation.

H. Complete each measure with *one* note.

I. Write the correct meter signature for each of these measures. In some instances, there is more than one correct answer.

J. Rewrite and correct the notation. Do not remove or change the pitch of any note.

1. Instrumental

2. Instrumental

3. Instrumental

4. Vocal

How I wish I were with you!

5. Piano

K. On a separate sheet of paper, rewrite the following excerpt, raising each tone one half step through the use of accidentals.

Schumann: "Trällerliedchen" (Humming Song) from *Album for the Young*, op. 68, no. 3, mm. 1–4.

L. On a separate sheet of paper, rewrite the above excerpt, lowering each tone one half step by using the proper accidentals.

M. On a separate sheet of paper, rewrite the above excerpt, changing the meter signature to $\frac{4}{8}$. Make sure the $\frac{4}{8}$ measures contain the same number of notes as the $\frac{4}{4}$ measures.

Review

You will find sections labeled "Review" near the end of each chapter in this Workbook/Anthology. The purpose of these sections is to provide a list of specific activities to improve your understanding of and fluency with the materials of the chapter. Music theory study is different from other academic classes you have had, and the study skills you have acquired there may not work in this class. Reading the chapter again or studying the areas you highlighted on first reading will not suffice. These materials must be practiced on a regular basis until they become second nature to you. If you take time to work on the following suggestions, you will find your knowledge and skills improving, and you will be on your way to success.

1. Look at the list of topics at the head of the chapter (page 3 in the textbook). Try to recall as specifically as possible the content of each of the sections. If any topics seem unclear to you, target those sections for careful study.

2. Sit at a piano keyboard. Play random white keys. For each key played, name the note, the solfeggio syllable, and the specific octave identification.

3. Take a piece of music. Look at each note and name the half step above and below that note.

4. Look in the anthology section beginning on page 167. Examine the meter signature of each piece and identify it as simple meter or compound meter. Can you locate a division of the beat? A subdivision? Are there any irregular divisions?

5. Take a piece of music. Copy it on a blank piece of paper. In the days before copy machines, musicians regularly copied music, and it is said that many great composers learned their craft by copying other composers' music. You must learn to produce clear, legible manuscript, and copying music and comparing your work with the original is good practice. Even though we now have computer programs to create music manuscript, you can still learn a lot about music notation by copying music by hand.

Test Yourself 1

Answers are on page 235.

1. Write the letter name of each of the following notes and indicate the octave identification.

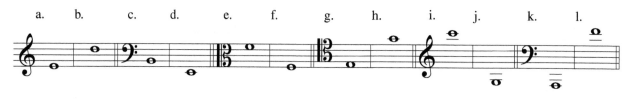

  a.   b.   c.   d.   e.   f.   g.   h.   i.   j.   k.   l.

___ ___ ___ ___ ___ ___ ___ ___ ___ ___ ___ ___

2. Find the pairs of enharmonic equivalents among the following 10 notes.

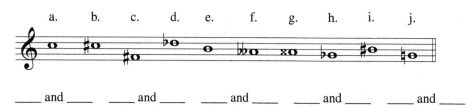

  a.   b.   c.   d.   e.   f.   g.   h.   i.   j.

____ and ____   ____ and ____   ____ and ____   ____ and ____   ____ and ____

3. Find the errors in notation in each measure below.

4. Name the note one half step above each of the following notes.

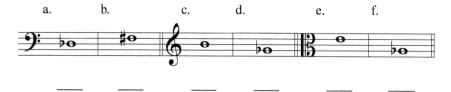

  a.   b.   c.   d.   e.   f.

___ ___ ___ ___ ___ ___

CHAPTER 2
Scales, Tonality, Key, Modes

A. Add the accidentals (on the staff, to individual notes) needed to form each scale.

1. D major

2. A♭ major

3. B ascending melodic minor

4. C♯ natural minor

5. G♯ harmonic minor

6. E♭ major

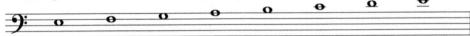

7. B♭ ascending melodic minor

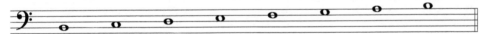

8. G♭ major

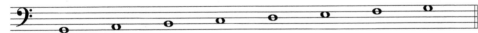

9. G harmonic minor

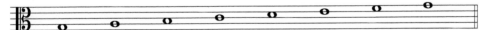

10. F ascending melodic minor

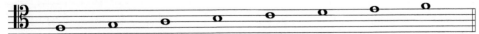

B. Each tone below is described as a degree in a particular *major* scale. Name the major key.

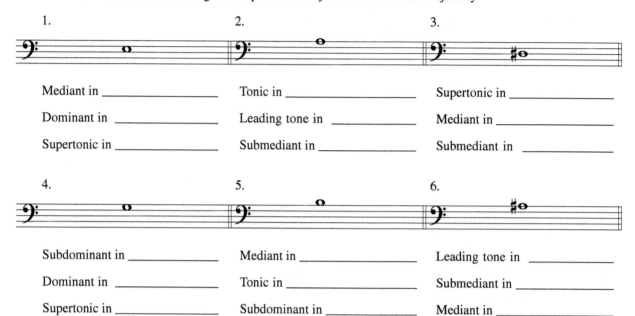

1.

Mediant in _____

Dominant in _____

Supertonic in _____

2.

Tonic in _____

Leading tone in _____

Submediant in _____

3.

Supertonic in _____

Mediant in _____

Submediant in _____

4.

Subdominant in _____

Dominant in _____

Supertonic in _____

5.

Mediant in _____

Tonic in _____

Subdominant in _____

6.

Leading tone in _____

Submediant in _____

Mediant in _____

C. Each tone below is described as a degree in a particular *natural* or *harmonic minor* scale. Name the minor key.

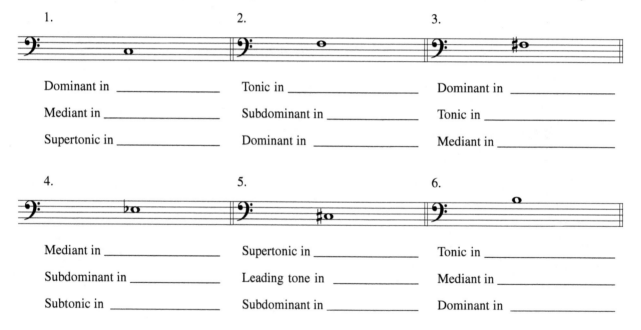

1.

Dominant in _____

Mediant in _____

Supertonic in _____

2.

Tonic in _____

Subdominant in _____

Dominant in _____

3.

Dominant in _____

Tonic in _____

Mediant in _____

4.

Mediant in _____

Subdominant in _____

Subtonic in _____

5.

Supertonic in _____

Leading tone in _____

Subdominant in _____

6.

Tonic in _____

Mediant in _____

Dominant in _____

D. Write the key signature for each of the 10 following keys:

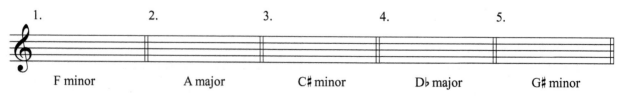

1. F minor   2. A major   3. C# minor   4. Db major   5. G# minor

E. Match the column on the right with that on the left by writing the number representing the correct answer in each blank.

1. Parallel minor of F♯ major   C major   _____

2. Relative minor of F♯ major   B♭ major   _____

3. Enharmonic with A♭ minor   F♯ minor   _____

4. Relative major of G minor   D♯ minor   _____

5. Parallel minor of A♭ major   C minor   _____

6. Enharmonic with F♯ major   E major   _____

7. Relative major of C♯ minor   G major   _____

8. Parallel major of G minor   G♯ minor   _____

9. Parallel major of C minor   G♭ major   _____

10. Relative minor of E♭ major   A♭ minor   _____

F. Rewrite the following, adding or subtracting accidentals to conform to the scale requested.

Brahms: Symphony no. 1 in C Major, op. 68, IV: Allegro, mm. 62–65.

1. Natural minor

2. Harmonic minor

3. Melodic minor (ascending or descending form where appropriate)

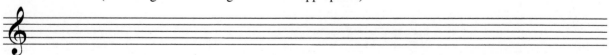

G. Each of the following melodies is based on one of the scales listed here. Write the name of the proper scale in the blank provided.

Scales: Major   Natural minor   Harmonic minor   Melodic minor   Pentatonic   Chromatic   Whole tone

1. _____

2. _____

3. _____

4. _____

5. _____

6. _____

7. _____

8. _____

9. _____

10. _____

H. Add the correct accidentals to form the mode requested.

1. Phrygian mode

2. Dorian mode

3. Mixolydian mode

4. Lydian mode

5. Aeolian mode

I. Add or subtract accidentals to change these melodies to the mode requested.

1. Dorian mode

2. Lydian mode

3. Mixolydian mode

4. Phrygian mode

5. Aeolian mode

J. In each of the six melodies that follow:
1. Write the pitch inventory, always beginning with A.
2. Examine the melody for clues to a possible tonic note, especially observing:
   a. Direction of the melody pointing to a tonic
   b. Strong intervallic relationships stressing a central tone
   c. Cadence emphasizing a central tone
3. Go back and examine the pitch inventory to see if it can be arranged into a scale according to your findings for instruction 2.
4. Arrange the pitch inventory into a scale with the tonic as the first pitch.
5. Examine your scale to see if it fits a pattern of a mode (for example, Dorian, Phrygian), a key (major or minor), or one of the other scales introduced in Chapter 2.
6. Enter this information as requested.

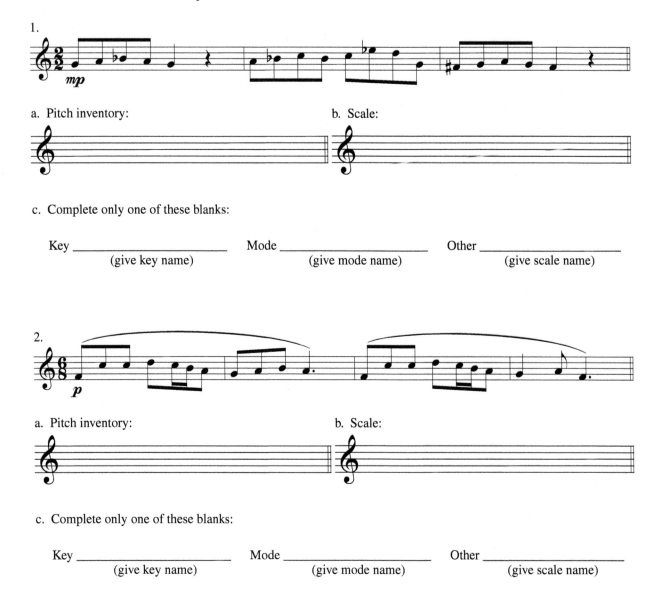

1.

a. Pitch inventory: b. Scale:

c. Complete only one of these blanks:

Key _____ Mode _____ Other _____
         (give key name)   (give mode name)   (give scale name)

2.

a. Pitch inventory: b. Scale:

c. Complete only one of these blanks:

Key _____ Mode _____ Other _____
         (give key name)   (give mode name)   (give scale name)

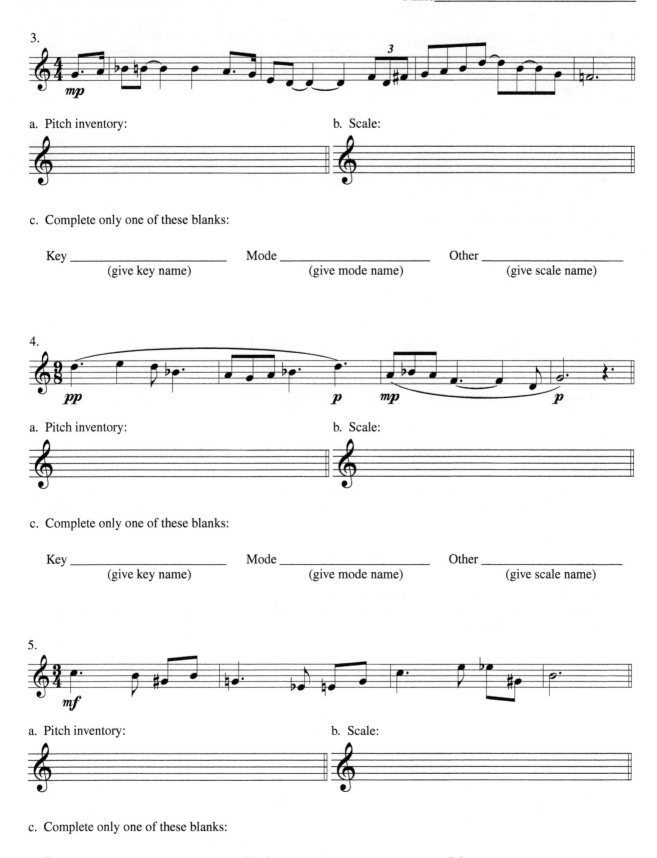

3.

a. Pitch inventory: b. Scale:

c. Complete only one of these blanks:

Key _____   Mode _____   Other _____
        (give key name)   (give mode name)   (give scale name)

4.

a. Pitch inventory: b. Scale:

c. Complete only one of these blanks:

Key _____   Mode _____   Other _____
        (give key name)   (give mode name)   (give scale name)

5.

a. Pitch inventory: b. Scale:

c. Complete only one of these blanks:

Key _____   Mode _____   Other _____
        (give key name)   (give mode name)   (give scale name)

6.

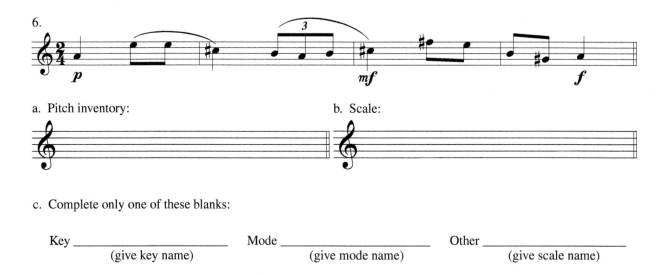

a. Pitch inventory:

b. Scale:

c. Complete only one of these blanks:

Key _____   Mode _____   Other _____
           (give key name)   (give mode name)   (give scale name)

K. Refer to "Rumanian Folk Song" from *Sketches*, op. 9b, no. 5 on page 178, and Bagatelle, op. 6, no. 5, by Béla Bartók (1881–1945) on page 177.
1. Play or sing the melody only and determine the type of scale or mode used.
2. Examine the accompaniment and circle all pitches that do not conform to the scale or mode of the composition.

Review

1. Starting on C, write the key signature for the major scale on each half step. Check your work by referring to Figure 2.8 in the text (page 31). Now do the same for minor scales. Check your work using Figure 2.20 on page 38.

2. At the piano keyboard, play the major scale and the three forms of the minor scales beginning on each pitch. Name the notes using letter names as you play each scale.

3. Take a single note. Make it the tonic, the supertonic, the mediant, the subdominant, the dominant, the submediant, and the leading tone of a major scale. Now make it the subtonic of a minor scale. Choose another note and repeat the exercise.

4. Name the major and minor scale for each of the key signatures from seven sharps through seven flats.

5 . For each composition in the Anthology look at the key signature and name the major and minor scale for that key signature. (Can you tell if the piece is in a major or a minor key?)

6. Work with a friend in spelling the major scales and the three forms of the minor scales. Take turns asking for a scale and check each other's work. See who can spell the most scales without making an error.

7. Look at the list of topics at the beginning of the chapter and review any areas for which you cannot remember specific details.

8. Using familiar melodies or melodies from your sight-singing book, do a pitch inventory of several melodies. Can you identify the scale from your inventory and by examining the melody?

9. If you have computer software available for the major and minor scales, use it to review.

Test Yourself 2

Answers are on page 235.

1. Identify each of the following scales (major, natural minor, harmonic minor, melodic minor).

a.   b.

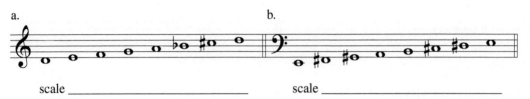

    scale _____   scale _____

c.   d.

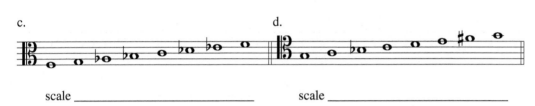

    scale _____   scale _____

2. Name the major and the minor scale for each of the following key signatures.

a.   b.   c.   d.

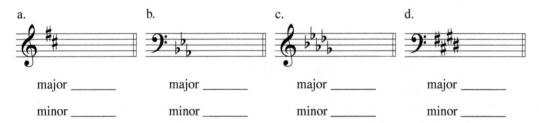

   major _____   major _____   major _____   major _____

   minor _____   minor _____   minor _____   minor _____

3. Each of the following groups of notes is part of two major scales. Name the two scales.

a.   b.   c.   d.

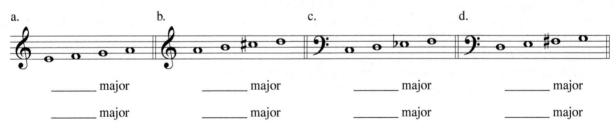

   _____ major   _____ major   _____ major   _____ major

   _____ major   _____ major   _____ major   _____ major

4. Give the letter name for each of the following scale degrees:

   a.   Supertonic of A major   _____

   b.   Submediant of D harmonic minor   _____

   c.   Subdominant of B♭ melodic minor   _____

   d.   Subtonic of F♯ natural minor   _____

5. Name the following keys:

    a. The relative minor of Db major   _____

    b. The relative major of B minor   _____

    c. The parallel major of C# minor   _____

    d. Enharmonic with Gb major   _____

6. Identify each of the following scales (minor, pentatonic, chromatic, whole tone).

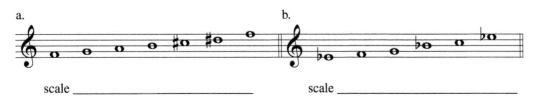

    scale _____   scale _____

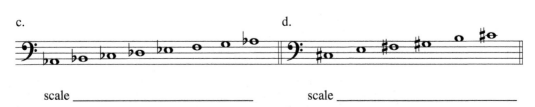

    scale _____   scale _____

7. Identify each of the following modes (Dorian, Phrygian, Lydian, Mixolydian).

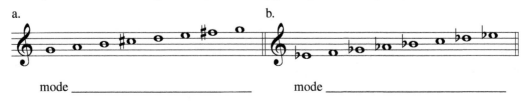

    mode _____   mode _____

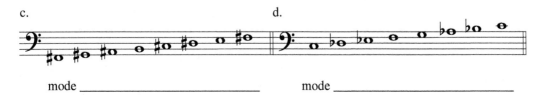

    mode _____   mode _____

CHAPTER 3
Intervals and Transposition

A. Write the name of each interval on the blank provided.

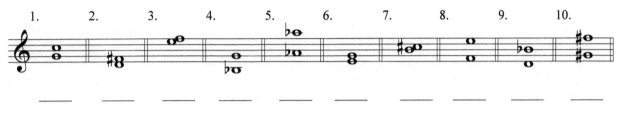

1.   2.   3.   4.   5.   6.   7.   8.   9.   10.

_____ _____ _____ _____ _____ _____ _____ _____ _____ _____

11. 12. 13. 14. 15. 16. 17. 18. 19. 20.

_____ _____ _____ _____ _____ _____ _____ _____ _____ _____

B. Write the requested interval both *above* and *below* the given tone.

1. (Ex.) 2.   3.   4.   5.   6.   7.   8.   9.   10.

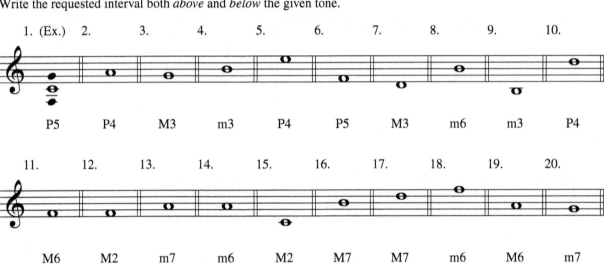

P5   P4   M3   m3   P4   P5   M3   m6   m3   P4

11. 12. 13. 14. 15. 16. 17. 18. 19. 20.

M6   M2   m7   m6   M2   M7   M7   m6   M6   m7

21. 22. 23. 24. 25. 26. 27. 28. 29. 30.

P5   P4   M3   m3   M3   P4   P5   P4   M3   m3

31. 32. 33. 34. 35. 36. 37. 38. 39. 40.

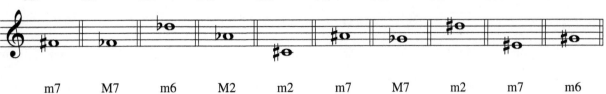

m7   M7   m6   M2   m2   m7   M7   m2   m7   m6

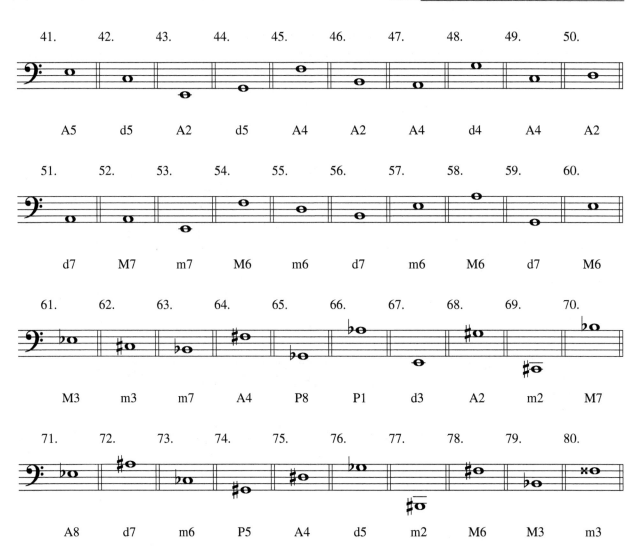

41. 42. 43. 44. 45. 46. 47. 48. 49. 50.

A5   d5   A2   d5   A4   A2   A4   d4   A4   A2

51. 52. 53. 54. 55. 56. 57. 58. 59. 60.

d7   M7   m7   M6   m6   d7   m6   M6   d7   M6

61. 62. 63. 64. 65. 66. 67. 68. 69. 70.

M3   m3   m7   A4   P8   P1   d3   A2   m2   M7

71. 72. 73. 74. 75. 76. 77. 78. 79. 80.

A8   d7   m6   P5   A4   d5   m2   M6   M3   m3

C. Here are some additional intervals to write. Write the requested interval *above* the given note. Below the given note write and label the inversion.

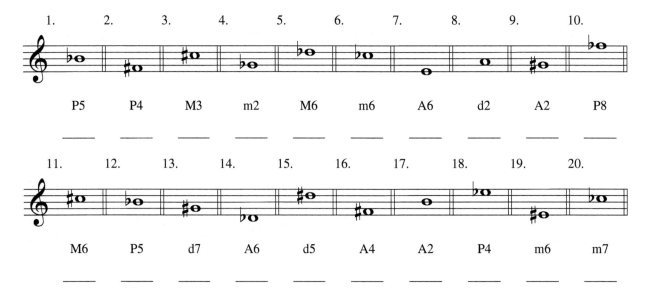

1. 2. 3. 4. 5. 6. 7. 8. 9. 10.

P5   P4   M3   m2   M6   m6   A6   d2   A2   P8

____ ____ ____ ____ ____ ____ ____ ____ ____ ____

11. 12. 13. 14. 15. 16. 17. 18. 19. 20.

M6   P5   d7   A6   d5   A4   A2   P4   m6   m7

____ ____ ____ ____ ____ ____ ____ ____ ____ ____

D. Below is a series of 32 compound intervals (intervals exceeding an octave in size).
  1. First, reduce each compound interval to its simple equivalent by transposing the upper note down an octave (or two octaves when needed) to make the interval less than an octave in size.
  2. When the compound interval has been reduced to a simple interval write its name (P5, M6, A4, etc.) in the blank provided. Numbers 23–32 are more difficult than the first 22.

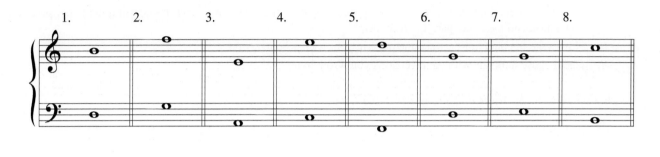

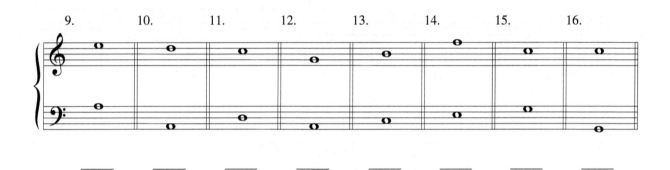

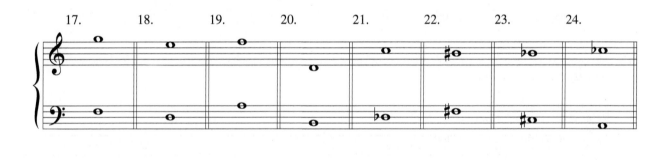

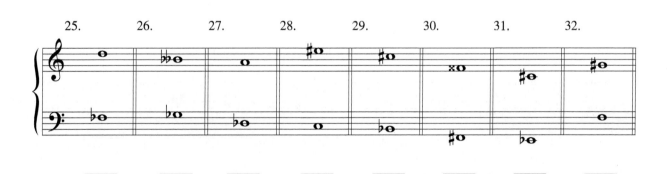

E. The following is a canon by J. S. Bach (1685–1750) from *The Musical Offering*.

1. Write the harmonic intervals between the tones of this two-voice composition. Blanks are provided between the staves.

2. When the interval size exceeds an octave, simply subtract the octave (example: a 10th becomes a 3rd when the octave is subtracted). Intervals that exceed an octave are called *compound intervals*.

3. Write the inversion of each interval below the staff in the blanks provided.

4. When this is completed, rewrite the excerpt on a separate sheet of score paper, transposing the upper part down one octave and the lower part up one octave.

5. Now write the intervals between the parts in your transposed version.

6. Check these intervals with the inversions you wrote in no. 3 above.

Bach: Canon from *The Musical Offering*, BWV 1079, mm. 1–7.

F. Refer to "Rigaudon" from *Pièces de Clavecin* by François Couperin (1668–1733) on page 192.

1. In the blanks below each double staff, indicate the interval between the lowest- and highest-sounding voices.

2. All the intervals are compound (greater than an octave), so it will be necessary to subtract the octave or octaves to reduce them to simple (less than an octave) intervals.

3. The first five intervals are provided to illustrate the procedure.

G. Here is a melody by Strauss. Indicate the melodic intervals (the intervals between the tones of the melody).

R. Strauss: *Don Juan*, op. 20.

H. In this group of nine intervals there are three enharmonic pairs. Find the pairs of enharmonic intervals.

Numbers _____ and _____ are enharmonic intervals.

Numbers _____ and _____ are enharmonic intervals.

Numbers _____ and _____ are enharmonic intervals.

I. Transpose the following melodies the interval indicated. Include the correct key signature for each transposition.

1. Rameau: Menuet en Rondeau in C Major, mm. 1–4.

Transpose down a M6:

2. Bach: Bourrée from Suite in E Minor, BWV 996, mm. 1–4.

Transpose down a P4:

3. Glinka: Intermezzo in B Minor, mm. 1–4.

Transpose up a M2:

Name_____

J. Rewrite the following melody for each of the instruments named below.
1. The melody is written at concert pitch (actual pitch).
2. Each instrument is to play the same pitches indicated in the melody. Thus, transposition is necessary in all cases except for no. 6.
3. Be sure to include the proper key signatures.

The melody:

1. Clarinet in B♭

2. Clarinet in A

3. English Horn

4. Horn in F

5. Trumpet in D

6. Viola (To place the melody into a better range for the viola, write the notes an octave lower than printed.)

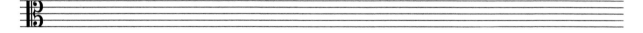

7. Alto Saxophone

K. Following are the first eight measures of the Menuetto from Symphony no. 39 by Mozart. On the blank staves that follow, rewrite the clarinet, horn, and trumpet parts in concert pitch (actual pitch). Refer to Appendix E on page 381 in the text as needed to find the correct transposition.

Mozart: Symphony no. 39 in E-flat Major, K. 543, III: Menuetto, mm. 1–8.

1. Clarinet in B♭

2. Horn in E♭

3. Trumpet in E♭

L. Below are the opening measures to Symphony no. 38, the "Prague Symphony," by Mozart. On the blank staves below, rewrite the horn, trumpet, and string bass parts in concert pitch.

Mozart: Symphony no. 38 in D Major ("Prague"), K. 543, I: Adagio, mm. 1–4.

1. Horns in D

2. Trumpets in D

3. Double Bass

M. Rewrite the following melody for each of the instruments named below.
   1. The melody is a B♭ clarinet part as the clarinetist would play it from a score. Thus, it is not written at concert pitch.
   2. Be sure to transpose the melody so each instrument will play the same pitches as those played by the clarinetist.
   3. Include the proper key signature for each instrument.

Clarinet in B♭

1. Oboe

2. Trumpet in B♭

3. Horn in F

4. Alto Saxophone

Review

1. Look at the list of concepts at the beginning of the chapter in the text. Define each term in your own words and check your definition with the book.
2. Take one note and name each of the following intervals above that note: m2, M2, A2, m3, M3, P4, A4, d5, P5, A5, m6, M6, A6, m7, M7. Now name the same list of intervals below that note. Now select a new note and repeat the exercise.
3. Sit at a piano keyboard and play two tones at random. Name the interval. Spell one of the tones enharmonically and rename the interval. Move the lower tone up an octave, now name the interval.
4. Select a major scale. Identify all pairs of scale degrees that are a M2 apart, spelling each. Repeat this process for each interval type (refer to item 2 above). This exercise should also be practiced using a minor scale.
5. Select a major scale, name the interval between each scale degree and the remaining scale degrees. In the same way, name the intervals in the three forms of the minor scale.
6. Look at a piece of music. Name the interval between each note in the melody.
7. Work with a friend on spelling intervals.
8. Use computer software if it is available.

Test Yourself 3

Answers are on page 236.

1. Name the seven consonant intervals.

   a. _____ b. _____ c. _____ d. _____ e. _____ f. _____ g. _____

2. Identify each of the following intervals.

   ____ ____ ____ ____ ____ ____

3. Name the inversion of each of the intervals in question 2.

   a. _____ b. _____ c. _____ d. _____ e. _____ f. _____

4. Identify the intervals between the two voices below.

5. Name the note that is the requested interval *above* each of the following notes:

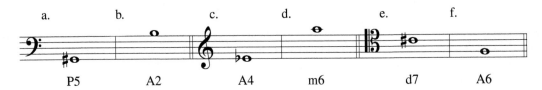

   P5   A2   A4   m6   d7   A6

6. Name the note that is the requested interval *below* each of the notes in question 5.

   a. _____ b. _____ c. _____ d. _____ e. _____ f. _____

CHAPTER 4
Chords

A. Indicate in the blanks below the type of triad shown. Use the following abbreviations:

M = major
m = minor
A = augmented
d = diminished

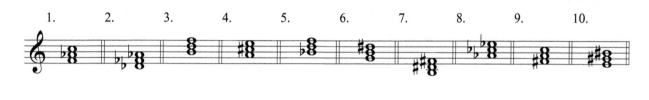

1. _____ 2. _____ 3. _____ 4. _____ 5. _____ 6. _____ 7. _____ 8. _____ 9. _____ 10. _____

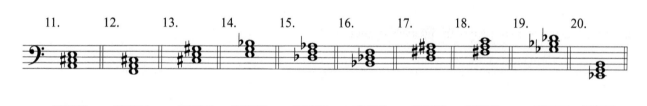

11. _____ 12. _____ 13. _____ 14. _____ 15. _____ 16. _____ 17. _____ 18. _____ 19. _____ 20. _____

B. Write each requested triad with the given note as the root (M = major, m = minor, A = augmented, d = diminished).

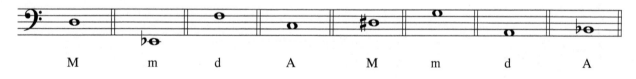

   M   m   d   A   M   m   d   A

C. Write each requested triad with the given note as the third (M = major, m = minor, A = augmented, d = diminished).

   d   d   m   m   M   M   A   A

D. Write each requested triad with the given note as the fifth (M = major, m = minor, A = augmented, d = diminished).

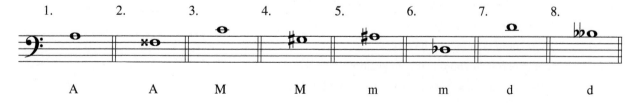

   A   A   M   M   m   m   d   d

E. In the blanks provided, write the macro analysis symbol for each of the triads given below. Use the following guidelines for writing the letter symbols:

        Major = Capital letter
        Minor = Lowercase letter
     Diminished = Lowercase letter plus °
     Augmented = Capital letter plus +

    ____   ____   ____   ____   ____   ____   ____   ____   ____   ____

F. Refer to the Schumann's "Ein Choral" ("A Chorale") from *Album for the Young*, op. 68, no. 4, on page 228.

    1. Indicate the letter name of each triad using the following symbols:

              Major = Capital letter
              Minor = Lowercase letter
          Diminished = Lowercase letter plus °
          Augmented = Capital letter plus +

    2. Ignore the circled notes. They are not considered part of the triads.

    3. This composition contains a few 7th chords (chords with an added 3rd above the 5th). These chords have been analyzed for you.

G. Refer to Handel's "Hallelujah" chorus on page 198. Name all the chords in each of the measures indicated below. Use the same symbols to indicate chords as in section E above. If a chord is used more than once in a measure, you need not name each appearance.

        Measure 4 _____

        Measure 5 _____

        Measure 6 _____

        Measure 7 _____

        Measure 8 _____

        Measure 9 _____

        Measure 10 _____

H. Refer to Mason's "Joy to the World" on page 216.

    1. Write a Roman numeral analysis and indicate the position:

        6 — if chord is in first inversion

        $^6_4$ — if chord is in second inversion

        no numbers — if chord is in root position

    2. Ignore the circled notes. They are not considered triad pitches.

I. The following are four-part arrangements of triads.
    1. On the staff below each chord, write out the triad in root position (see the example).
    2. In the first blank, write the type of triad (M = major, m = minor, d = diminished, and A = augmented).
    3. In the lower blank, write the sign indicating the arrangement of the four-part harmony:

    ^{6} — if chord is in first inversion
    $^6_4$ — if chord is in second inversion
    no numbers — if chord is in root position

J. Here is an excerpt from a piano composition. Instead of being written in block chords, as in Exercise I on page 29, the harmony is arpeggiated (spread out in a linear fashion).

   1. In each blank, write the chord analysis using Roman numerals (as shown on pages 78–80 of the text). The following chords are used:

   $$i \qquad i_4^6 \qquad ii^{\circ 6} \qquad iv^6 \qquad iv_4^6 \qquad V \qquad V^6$$

   2. Note that there is one chord per measure until measure 7, which contains three chords.

E minor: _____ _____ _____ _____

_____ _____ _____ _____ _____ _____

K. Complete each chord according to figured-bass symbols. Use the simple position (the closest possible arrangement).

L. Complete each chord according to figured-bass symbols. Use the simple position (the closest possible arrangement).

Review

1. Take a single note. Spell one major, one minor, one augmented, and one diminished triad with that note as the root. Now make that note the third of each of the four triad qualities. Now make it the fifth of each triad quality. Choose another note and repeat the exercise.

2. Review the concepts listed at the beginning of the chapter in the text.

3. Choose a note and write the major scale and then a triad on each scale degree. Identify the quality of each triad and write the appropriate Roman numeral below the chord. Repeat this exercise using the natural minor scale, the harmonic minor scale, and the melodic minor scale. Repeat this exercise using a different note.

4. Take a familiar hymn or look at the "Hallelujah" chorus from Handel's *Messiah* on page 198 in the Anthology. Examine the notes in the four parts on a given beat and identify a chord, if possible (there may be tones that are not part of the chords in this music, so don't be surprised if you can't always identify a chord). Identify the inversion for each chord you find.

5. Use computer software if it is available.

Test Yourself 4

Answers are on page 236.

1. Indicate the quality (major, minor, augmented, diminished) of each of the following triads:

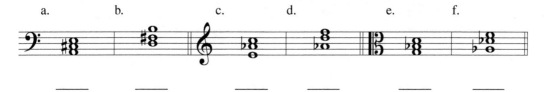

2. Give the macro analysis letter symbol for each of the triads above.

a. _____ b. _____ c. _____ d. _____ e. _____ f. _____

3. For each of the following chords, name the scale degree on which it is built, and give the correct Roman numeral. Indicate the inversions in the standard way.

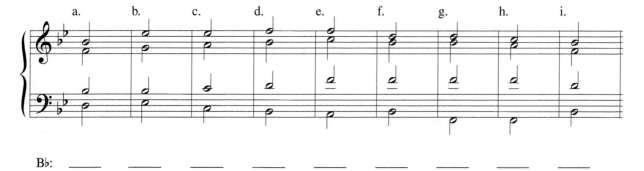

Bb: _____ _____ _____ _____ _____ _____ _____ _____ _____

4. Indicate the proper Roman numeral for the given chord if it occurs in each of the following keys:

   a. A♭ major: _____   b. G minor: _____   c. B♭ major: _____

   d. C minor: _____   e. E♭ major: _____   f. F minor: _____

5. Indicate the proper Roman numeral for the given chord if it occurs in each of the following keys:

   a. D major : _____   b. F♯ minor: _____   c. A major: _____

   d. E minor: _____   e. G major: _____   f. B minor: _____

6. Give the popular music symbol for each of the following triads.

   a. _____   b. _____   c. _____   d. _____   e. _____   f. _____

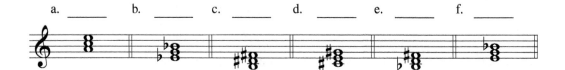

CHAPTER 5
Cadences and Nonharmonic Tones

A. Each of the following short excerpts ends with a cadence.

1. Write the Roman numeral analysis of each chord and indicate the position (^{6} if in first inversion, $^6_4$ if in second inversion, and no numbers if in root position).

2. Name the cadence using the following types:

Perfect authentic	Plagal
Imperfect authentic	Deceptive
Half	

1. _____   2. _____   3. _____

B♭: ___ ___ ___ ___   f: ___ ___ ___ ___   A: ___ ___ ___ ___

4. _____   5. _____   6. _____

e: ___ ___ ___ ___   g: ___ ___ ___ ___   b: ___ ___ ___ ___

7. _____   8. _____   9. _____

E: ___ ___ ___ ___   f♯: ___ ___ ___ ___   E♭: ___ ___ ___ ___

B. Refer to Nicolai's "Wachet auf, ruft uns die Stimme" on page 225. Each phrase ending is marked with a fermata and the key is indicated just before the cadence. Name the cadence of each phrase using the following cadence types:

Perfect authentic   Plagal
Imperfect authentic   Deceptive
Half

Measure Nos.   *Cadence Type*

4–5   _____

9–10   _____

13–14   _____

17–18   _____

20–21   _____

23–24   _____

25–26   _____

27–28   _____

31–32   _____

C. Rewrite each chord progression in the blank measure provided and add the requested nonharmonic tone.

1. Passing tone   2. Accented   3. Neighboring tone   4. Anticipation
                      passing tone   in soprano

5. Appoggiatura   6. 4–3 suspension   7. 7–6 suspension   8. Escape tone
   in soprano   in soprano

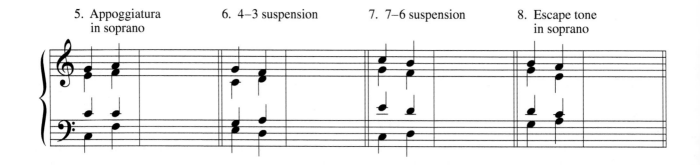

9. 2–3 suspension   10. Double   11. 4–3 suspension   12. 9–8 suspension
                passing tones   decorated   decorated

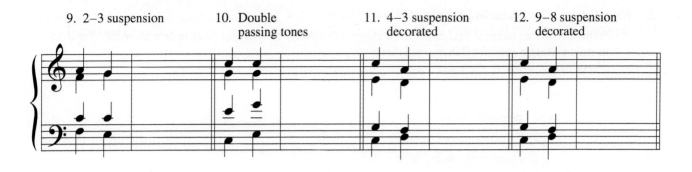

13. 9–8 suspension with   14. Double accented   15. Double   16. Retardation
     change of bass tone   neighboring tones   appoggiatura

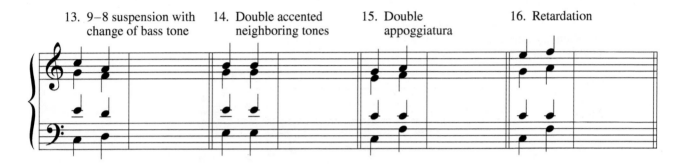

D. Following are two phrases of a chorale harmonized by Bach. The nonharmonic tones have been removed.

1. Provide a Roman numeral analysis of each chord, indicating also the position (^{6} if in first inversion, $^6_4$ if in second inversion, and no numbers if in root position).

2. Then, on the blank staff, rewrite the two phrases and add nonharmonic tones of your choice. Include at least two suspensions. If you wish to add escape tones, anticipations, or appoggiaturas, place them *only* in the soprano voice. Other nonharmonic tones can be added to any voice.

Bach: "Der Tag, der ist so freudenreich" ("This Day Is So Joyful"), BWV 294, mm. 1–4.

_____:_ _ _ _ _ _ _ _ _ _ _ _ _ _ _
Key

E. The following are examples of Bach chorales.

1. Write the Roman numeral analysis of each chord and indicate the position (^{6} if in first inversion, $^6_4$ if in second inversion, and no numbers if in root position).

2. Circle all nonharmonic tones and write the abbreviations representing the name nearby.

Unaccented passing tone = PT

Accented passing tone = $\overset{>}{\text{PT}}$

9–8 suspension = 9–8 SUS

2–3 suspension = 2–3 SUS

The first chord of each example is analyzed correctly for you.

1. "Lobt Gott, ihr Christen, allzugleich" ("Praise God, Ye Christians, All Together"), BWV 376, mm. 1–2.

A: I   ___ ___ ___ ___ ___ ___ ___

2. "Wo soll ich fliehen hin" ("Whither Am I to Flee"), BWV 89, mm. 1–2.

g: i   ___ ___ ___ ___ ___ ___

3. "Christe, du Beistand deiner Kreuzgemeinde" ("Christ, Thou Support of Thy Followers"), BWV 275, mm. 1–2.

d: i   ___ ___ ___ ___ ___ ___

4. "Liebster Jesu, wir sind hier" ("Dearest Jesus, We Are Here"), BWV 373, mm. 1–2.

G: I   ___   ___   ___   ___

5. "Seelen-Bräutigam" ("Bridegroom of the Soul"), BWV 409, mm. 1–2.

A: I   ___   ___   ___   ___

6. "Vater unser im Himmelreich" ("Our Father, Thou in Heaven Above"), BWV 416, mm. 1–2.

d: i   ___   ___   ___   ___   ___   ___

F.   Refer to "Herr, ich habe missgehandelt" by Johann Crüger (1598–1662) on page 193.

1.   In the keys indicated on the score, provide a Roman numeral for each chord and specify inverions (^{6} if in first inversion, $^6_4$ if in second inversion, and no numbers if in root position).

2.   Circle all nonharmonic tones and write the abbreviations representing the name nearby (PT for unaccented passing tones and 4–3 SUS for 4–3 suspensions).

3.   Each phrase ending is marked with a fermata. Name the cadence type at the end of each phrase (perfect authentic, imperfect authentic, half, plagal, or deceptive).

G. Following are 10 excerpts, most of which are taken from chorales harmonized by Johann Sebastian Bach.

1. Write the analysis of each chord in the blank below the staves.

2. Remember, if a triad contains a nonharmonic tone, analyze it as if the nonharmonic tone were not present— mentally replace the nonharmonic tone with the corresponding chord tone.

3. Circle each nonharmonic tone.

4. Write the abbreviation representing the nonharmonic tone near the circle (see the list that follows).

5. In these examples most of the nonharmonic tones will be of eighth-note value, but be careful not to overlook those of quarter-note value as well.

6. Note that the excerpts contain little more than a measure and are not to be considered complete musical ideas.

Nonharmonic Tone Types

Accented passing tone	$\overset{>}{PT}$	Unaccented passing tone	PT
Accented neighboring tone	$\overset{>}{NT}$	Unaccented neighboring tone	NT
9–8 suspension	9–8 SUS	Escape tone	ET
7–6 suspension	7–6 SUS	Anticipation	ANT
4–3 suspension	4–3 SUS	Changing tones	CT
2–3 suspension	2–3 SUS	Pedal Tone	PED
Appoggiatura	APP	Retardation	RE

Example:

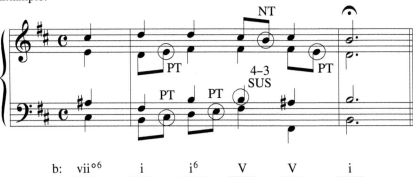

b: vii°⁶   i   i⁶   V   V   i

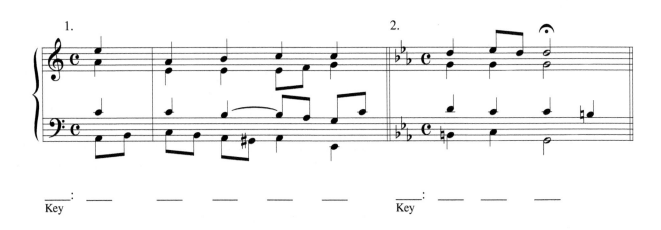

____: ___   ___   ___   ___   ___   ____: ___   ___   ___   ___
Key   Key

Name_____

Review

1. Play all the examples of cadences (Figures 5.1–5.5 on pages 98–99 in the text) on the piano and identify the features of each cadence as described in the accompanying text. Even if your piano skills are minimal, you will find this to be a helpful exercise.

2. Choose a few pieces from a collection of traditional and patriotic songs, a hymnal, or some similar music with clear phrases and a text.
   a. Find the key of each piece.
   b. Identify phrases by the given punctuation marks in the text.
   c. For each phrase identify the cadence type (authentic, plagal, etc.). Some phrases may be in keys other than the key of the piece as a whole, and you may not be able to identify the cadence type in every case.
   d. Examine the length of the phrases. Are all phrases the same length?

3. Look over the assignments you have completed for this chapter, paying particular attention to any difficulties you have encountered. Think through the process for completing each exercise.

4. Since you are likely to find problems similar to the assignments on an examination, work through some of the assignments that you were not required to complete during your study of the chapter. This will give you practice in working with the concepts of the chapter.

5. Play the examples of nonharmonic tones (Figures 5.12–5.34 on pages 102–111 of the text) on the piano. Pay particular attention to the three-tone pattern: *preceding tone, nonharmonic tone, and following tone.*

6. Study the summary of nonharmonic tones on page 111 of the text and memorize the approach and departure characteristics of each. Also memorize the list of abbreviations at the top of the chart. You will need these abbreviations to label nonharmonic tones in assignments and examinations.

7. Review the fundamentals (Chapters 1–5). You must review these basic facts on a regular basis and practice to achieve fluency. This repeated review will pay big dividends in future chapters.

Test Yourself 5

Answers are on pages 236–237.

Name the cadence type in the following short excerpts (each ending with a cadence). The cadence types are:

Perfect authentic	Plagal
Imperfect authentic	Deceptive
Half	

*Occasionally a 5th is missing. In this instance, analyze as if the 5th (B) were present.

Questions 16 and 17 refer to these examples:

16. Cadences:

    a.   The cadence at chord 3 is a(n) _____ cadence.

    b.   The cadence at chord 6 is a(n) _____ cadence.

    c.   The cadence at chord 9 is a(n) _____ cadence.

    d.   The cadence at chord 12 is a(n) _____ cadence.

    e.   The cadence at chord 15 is a(n) _____ cadence.

17. Nonharmonic tones:

    a.   The nonharmonic tone at chord 2 is a(n)_____.

    b.   The nonharmonic tone at chord 5 is a(n)_____.

    c.   The nonharmonic tone at chord 8 is a(n)_____.

    d.   The nonharmonic tone at chord 9 is a(n)_____.

    e.   The nonharmonic tone at chord 11 is a(n)_____.

    f.   The nonharmonic tone at chord 13 is a(n)_____.

    g.   The nonharmonic tone at chord 14 is a(n)_____.

CHAPTER 6
Melodic Organization

A. Following are 10 themes from symphonies by or attributed to Franz Joseph Haydn. Some are based on a motive and some are not.

1. Analyze each theme.
2. If the theme is based on a motive, circle the motive and each recurrence. Remember, a *motive* is a short melodic–rhythmic figure of just a few notes that is repeated (sometimes with modifications) enough times for the listener to be aware of its existence.
3. If the theme is not based on a motive, write "no" at the end of the score.

1. Symphony no. 103 in E-flat Major ("Drum Roll"), II, mm. 1–4.

2. Symphony no. 104 in D Major ("London"), I, mm. 17–20.

3. Symphony no. 104 in D Major ("London"), II: Andante, mm. 1–4.

4. Symphony no. 104 in D Major ("London"), IV: Finale, mm. 3–8.

5. Symphony in C Major ("Toy"). Attributed to Haydn, composed by Angerer.

6. Symphony in C Major ("Toy"). Attributed to Haydn, composed by Angerer.

7. Symphony in C Major ("Toy"). Attributed to Haydn, composed by Angerer.

8. Symphony in C Major ("Toy"). Attributed to Haydn, composed by Angerer.

9. Symphony no. 101 in D Major ("Clock"), III: Menuet, mm. 1–8.

10. Symphony no. 101 in D Major ("Clock"), IV: Finale, mm. 1–4.

B. Following are three phrases. Using the phrase relationships requested, add an additional phrase. Create a period when adding the parallel and contrasting phrases.

1. A major:

Modified repeated:

Parallel:

Contrasting:

2. C minor:

Modified repeated:

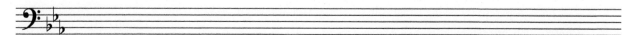

Parallel:

Contrasting:

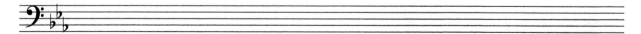

3. Tonality of D:

Modified repeated:

Parallel:

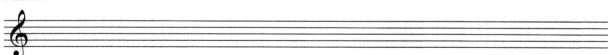

Contrasting:

C. Following are six melodies. Study each carefully and indicate the following.

1. A *phrase diagram*. Give the length of each phrase and its relationship to other phrases.

> *a* = The first phrase and any that are an exact repetition.
> *a'* = Any subsequent phrase that is a modified repeated version of the first phrase.
> *ap* = A phrase following *a* that is in parallel relationship to it.
> *b* = The next phrase after *a* that is contrasting to it (and any later phrases that are an exact repetition of *b*).
> *b'* = Any subsequent phrase that is a modified repeated version of the *b* phrase.
> *bp* = A phrase following *b* that is in parallel relationship to it.

Continue this procedure through *c*, *d*, *e*, and so on, as needed.

2. Point out any melodic organization you find, such as:

Sequence	Extension of a phrase
Motive	Compression of a phrase
Phrase member	Change of mode

3. The first melody is completed for you as a model.

(Ex.) Beethoven: Sonata in C Minor (*Pathétique*), op. 13, III: Rondo, mm. 1–12.

Phrase diagram:

Phrase Number	Phrase Length	Phrase Relationship
1	1–19	a
2	20–36	b
3	37–53	b

Melodic organization:

4–5 is a sequence with 6–7
9–12 is a sequence with 13–16
20–23 is a sequence with 24–27
30–32 is a sequence with 33–35

Same sequences in third phrase as in second.

Phrase member: 1–8
Phrase member: 9–19

Motive 20–22 appears 10 times in phrases 2 and 3.

1. Schubert: Sonata in A Major, D. 959, III: Rondo, mm. 1–16.

Phrase diagram (follow the model):

Melodic organization:

2. Schubert: Sonata in C Minor, D. 958, III: Allegro, mm. 1–16 (transposed and adapted).

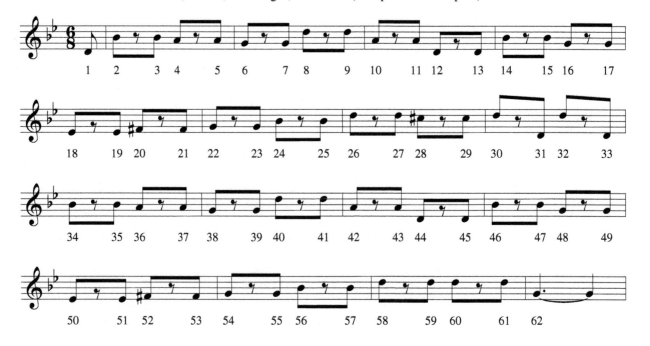

Phrase diagram (follow the model):

Melodic organization:

3. Haydn: Allegro Hob. III:73/4, mm. 1–16 (transposed and adapted).

Phrase diagram (follow the model):

Melodic organization:

4. Allegretto (England).

Phrase diagram (follow the model):

Melodic organization:

5. Andante con moto (Spain).

Phrase diagram (follow the model):

Melodic organization:

Name_____

6. Moderato (England).

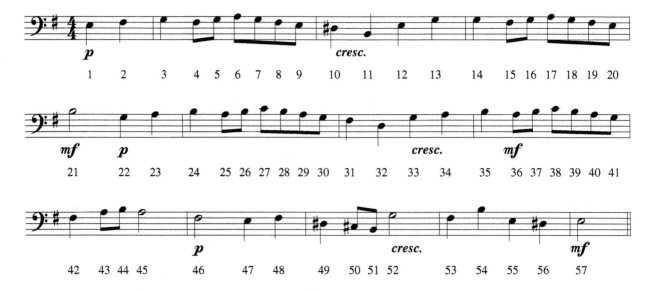

Phrase diagram (follow the model):

Melodic organization:

D. Expand the following phrase in the three ways requested.

Expansion at the beginning:

Internal expansion:

Cadential expansion:

E. Add a phrase with change in mode to the following phrase by Mozart.

Mozart: Symphony in G Minor, K. 183, III: Trio.

F. Make this two-measure melody into a four-measure phrase with a diatonic sequence.

G. Add a sequence segment to this two-measure melody. The added segment should be in C melodic minor and should end with an implied perfect authentic cadence (in C minor).

H. Add a sequence segment to this two-measure melody. The added segment should be in F major and should end with a perfect authentic cadence (in F major).

I. Continue this two-measure melody with a false sequence of two measures.

J. Refer to the Menuet and Trio from the Sonata in E Major, Hob. XVI:13 by Haydn on page 209.

1. Considering only the melody (highest voice), divide the composition into phrases. (Indications for twelve phrases are provided below, but alternate analyses may result in greater or fewer numbers.)

Phrase 1: measures _____ through _____   Phrase 7: measures _____ through _____

Phrase 2: measures _____ through _____   Phrase 8: measures _____ through _____

Phrase 3: measures _____ through _____   Phrase 9: measures _____ through _____

Phrase 4: measures _____ through _____   Phrase 10: measures _____ through _____

Phrase 5: measures _____ through _____   Phrase 11: measures _____ through _____

Phrase 6: measures _____ through _____   Phrase 12: measures _____ through _____

2. Indicate phrase relationships using letters as described in the text.

Phrase 1 _____   Phrase 4 _____   Phrase 7 _____   Phrase 10 _____

Phrase 2 _____   Phrase 5 _____   Phrase 8 _____   Phrase 11 _____

Phrase 3 _____   Phrase 6 _____   Phrase 9 _____   Phrase 12 _____

3. Indicate melodic repetitions (use measure numbers).

_____   _____   _____

_____   _____   _____

4. Indicate melodic sequences (use measure numbers and name the types of sequences).

_____   _____   _____

_____   _____   _____

K. Following are twelve excerpts from compositions. Analyze each melody in the following manner:

1. Indicate the *climax tone* with a box:

2. Indicate *ascent* pitches with an ascending line:

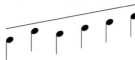

3. Show *descent* pitches with a descending line:

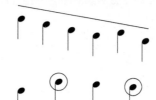

4. Circle notes of the tonic triad:

5. Number the scale pitches that conclude the phrase or period. Remember that scale degrees $\hat{3}$ and $\hat{2}$ must occur in that order but may be scattered throughout the excerpt, while $\hat{1}$ is always the final pitch of the phrase or period.

(Ex.) British Folk Song.

1. Allegro (England), mm. 1–8.

2. Monk: "Abide with Me" (hymn tune), mm. 9–16.

3. Schubert: Impromptu, op. 142, no. 2, D. 935, mm. 9–16.

4. Verdi: *Aïda*, act II, scene II: March, mm. 91–94.

5. Schubert: "Das Wandern" ("The Wandering") from *Die Schöne Müllerin* (The Miller's Beautiful Daughter), op. 25, no. 1, D. 795, mm. 5–7.

6. Schubert: Waltz, op. 9, no. 8, D. 365, mm. 1–8

7. Mozart: Magic Flute, act I, no. 8: Finale, mm. 303–310.

8. Mendelssohn: *Ein Sommernactstraum* (A Midsummer Night's Dream), op. 21, no. 5, Allegro molto comodo, mm. 148–155.

9. Russian Folk Song.

G:

10. German Folk Song.

Eb:

Review

1. This chapter introduces many terms that are used to describe the structure and organization of melody. Use the list of terms at the beginning of the chapter (page 119 of the text) as the basis for your review. Define each term for yourself and then check your definition with the appropriate section of the chapter.
2. Carefully examine the melodies that are given as examples in the chapter. Play or sing each melody and observe the labels applied to it.
3. Choose a few pieces from a collection of traditional and patriotic songs, a hymnal, or some similar music with clear phrases and a text.
    a. Find the key of each piece.
    b. Identify phrases by the given punctuation marks in the text.
    c. For each phrase identify the cadence type (authentic, plagal, etc.). Some phrases may be in keys other than the key of the piece as a whole, and you may not be able to identify the cadence type in every case.
    d. Examine the length of the phrases. Are all phrases the same length?
    e. Are the phrases grouped together into periods? How do you know? Are the periods parallel, contrasting, three-phrase, or double? How can you tell?
    f. Does the melody contain repeated melodic motives?
4. Look at music you are currently learning or that you have learned in the past. See if you can find an example of each of the elements of melody in the list at the beginning of the chapter.

Test Yourself 6

Answers are on page 237.

Following is an excerpt from a rondo by Wolfgang Amadeus Mozart (1756–91). A list of terms denoting compositional and formal devices follows it.

Examine the rondo carefully and locate an example of each of the terms listed. Then indicate the place in the composition where the example is found, using the line letters and beat numbers. (An example is provided.)

Mozart: Rondo K. 494, mm. 1–26.

Line E

Term	Can be found in (lines and numbers)
1. (Ex.) Internal extension of a phrase	Line A, numbers 5–8; line A, numbers 9–12
2. Parallel period	_____
3. A sequence of two segments of one-half measure each	_____
4. A retardation	_____
5. An appoggiatura	_____
6. A 4–3 suspension	_____
7. A sequence of two segments of one full measure each	_____
8. An authentic cadence in F major	_____
9. A half cadence in C major	_____
10. Exact melodic repetition	_____
11. A 7–6 suspension	_____
12. A lower neighboring tone	_____
13. An accented passing tone	_____
14. A second-inversion triad	_____
15. An imperfect authentic cadence in C major	_____
16. A phrase member	_____
17. A phrase extension near the beginning	_____
18. A set of contrasting phrases (period)	_____

Questions 19–21 refer to the "Lullaby" by Brahms:

Brahms: "Lullaby," op. 49, no. 4.

19. Divide this melody into phrases. The melody consists of _____ phrases.

20. Examine the phrases for period construction. This melody contains _____ period(s).

21. Describe the period(s) by type (parallel period, contrasting period, three-phase period, double period).

22. Analyze the following melody using the symbols given below:

Climax tone ☐

Ascent /

Descent \

Tonic triad ◯

Scale pitches that conclude the phrase or period $\hat{3}$ $\hat{2}$ $\hat{1}$

German Folk Song.

CHAPTER 7
Texture and Textural Reduction

A. Refer to Beethoven's Sonata in E-flat Major, op. 31, no. 3, on page 181.

   1. Examine the opening section of this work (measures 1–9A).

   2. The texture type is _____.

   3. Label the elements of the texture in measures 1–9A using the following labels:

   > PM   = Primary melody
   > SM   = Secondary melody
   > PSM = Parallel supporting melody
   > SS   = Static support
   > RS   = Rhythmic support
   > HRS = Harmonic and rhythmic support

B. Refer to Handel's Gigue from Suite no. 7 in B-flat Major, G. 33, on page 197.

   1. The texture type is _____.

   2. Label the elements of the texture throughout the composition using the labels in section A above.

C. Refer to Mozart's Piano Sonata in A Major, K. 331, on page 221.

   1. Examine measures 1–8 and identify the texture type. The texture is _____.

   2. Label the elements in the texture in measures 1–8 using the labels in section A above.

D. Refer to Schumann's "Fröhlicher Landmann" ("Happy Farmer") from *Album for the Young*, op. 68, no. 10 on page 230.

   1. The texture type is _____.

   2. Label the elements of the texture throughout the composition using the labels in section A above.

E. Refer to Handel's "Hallelujah!" from *Messiah*, on page 198.

   1. This work exhibits several texture types. Examine the sections listed below and identify the texture type of each section.

	Texture Type		*Texture Type*
Measures 4–11	_____	Measures 41–43	_____
Measures 12–14	_____	Measures 69–73	_____
Measures 22–32	_____	Measures 90–94	_____
Measures 33–41	_____		

   2. Do a textural analysis of the entire work, using the labels in section A above.

F. Refer to Haydn's Sonata in E Minor, Hob. XVI:34, on page 212.

   1. Determine the harmonic rhythm by playing the piece or listening to a recording.

   2. Do a harmonic reduction of the left hand (there are no nonharmonic tones until measure 15) and write the chords on the staff provided. Make sure to use proper rhythmic values.

Review

1. The four basic texture types and the seven textural elements are the most important concepts of this chapter. Review the discussion of each of these concepts, paying careful attention to the musical examples. In the discussion of textural elements (pages 151–155 in the text) the examples are analyzed. Carefully examine the labels and see if you understand the reason for each.

2. You should begin to look at the music you are performing to determine the texture type and relationship of textural elements. If you play a "one-line" instrument, this may be somewhat difficult, but you can use your ears or examine scores. You will find it very helpful to know how the lines you play fit into the texture. In many cases this information will assist you in interpretation. For instance, this information will alert you to bring out your part when it is the primary melody (PM), or to subordinate it when it is a secondary melody (SM) or a part of harmonic and rhythmic support (HRS).

3. The technique of harmonic reduction of accompaniment figures described on pages 155–156 of the text will be extremely valuable to you in later musical analysis in this class. Practice this technique, using the examples in the text, the assignments, and compositions in the anthology section of this workbook.

Test Yourself 7

Answers are on page 238.

Questions 1–4 refer to the four musical excerpts that follow.

1. Examine the four excerpts, which contain the four basic texture types described in the chapter. Identify the texture types and fill in the blanks below:

    monophonic texture _____.

    polyphonic texture _____.

    homophonic texture _____.

    homorhythmic texture _____.

2. Each excerpt has one or more parts labeled with numbers (1–7). Identify the textural elements and fill in the blanks below (you will not find an example of every textural element):

    Primary melody (PM) _____.

    Secondary melody (SM) _____.

    Parallel supporting melody (PSM) _____.

    Static support (SS) _____.

    Harmonic support (HS) _____.

    Rhythmic support (RS) _____.

    Harmonic rhythmic support (HRS) _____.

3. The thinnest texture is example _____.

4. The thickest texture is example _____.

a. Morley: "Sing We and Chant It," mm. 9–16.

b. Handel: "Comfort Ye" from *Messiah*, mm. 15–17.

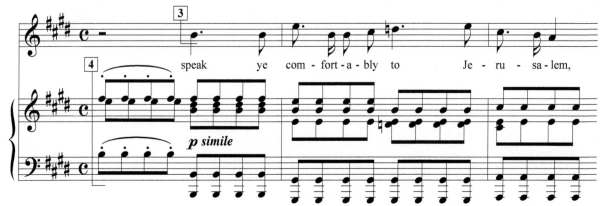

c. Haydn: Quartet, op. 76, no. 3, II: Poco adagio, mm. 21–22.

d. Debussy: Prelude to *The Afternoon of a Faun*, mm. 1–4.

5. Write a harmonic reduction for the bass clef (left-hand) portion of the following excerpt. The harmonic rhythm is given and nonharmonic tones have been circled.

Beethoven: Sonata in C Minor, op. 13, III: Allegro, mm. 1–8.

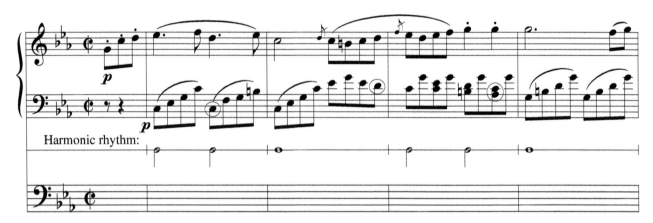

6. The right hand part in the preceding example is _____ (textural element).

   The left-hand part is _____ (textural element).

   The excerpt is an example of _____ texture (texture type).

CHAPTER 8
Species Counterpoint

A. Following are two cantus firmus melodies.
1. Compose a counterpoint in first species above each cantus firmus using the principles in Chapter 8.
2. Compose a counterpoint in first species below each cantus firmus using the principles in Chapter 8.
3. Pay particular attention to proper beginnings and endings, as shown on pages 169–170 of the text.
4. Make sure your counterpoint observes all the principles on pages 170–172 of the text.
5. Analyze the harmonic intervals. Write the interval number between your counterpoint and the cantus firmus.

Cantus firmus 1a

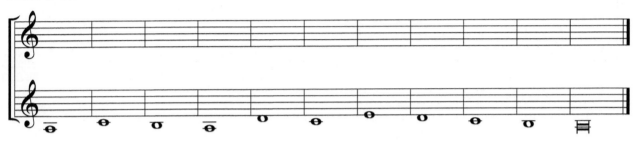

Cantus firmus 1b

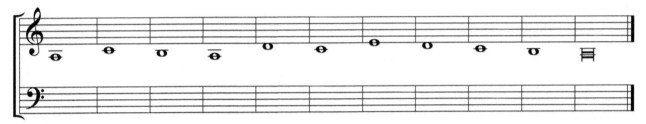

Cantus firmus 2a

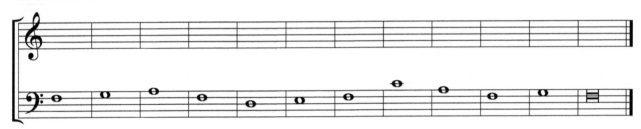

Cantus firmus 2b

B. Following are two cantus firmus melodies.
1. Compose a counterpoint in second species above each cantus firmus using the principles in Chapter 8.
2. Compose a counterpoint in second species below each cantus firmus using the principles in Chapter 8.
3. Pay particular attention to proper beginnings and endings, as shown on pages 172–173 of the text.
4. Make sure your counterpoint observes all the principles on pages 173–174 of the text.
5. Analyze the harmonic intervals. Write the interval number between your counterpoint and the cantus firmus.
6. Circle all numbers representing dissonances (2, 4, 7, 9, and d5). Make sure each dissonance appears as an unaccented passing tone.

Cantus firmus 1a

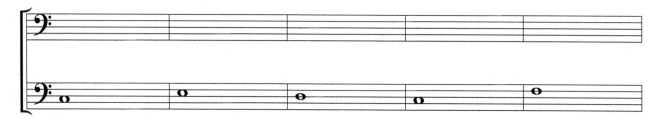

Cantus firmus 1b

Cantus firmus 2a

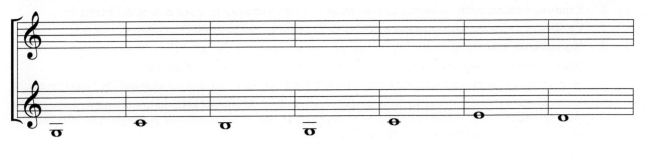

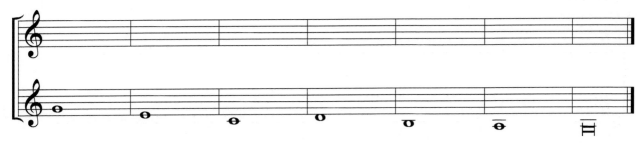

Cantus firmus 2b

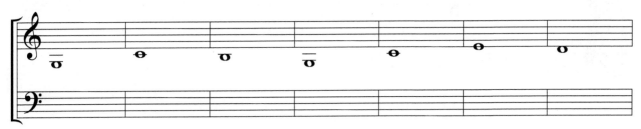

C. Following are two cantus firmus melodies.
1. Compose a counterpoint in third species above each cantus firmus using the principles in Chapter 8.
2. Compose a counterpoint in third species below each cantus firmus using the principles in Chapter 8.
3. Pay particular attention to proper beginnings and endings, as shown on page 175 of the text.
4. Make sure your counterpoint observes all the principles on pages 175–177 of the text.
5. Analyze the harmonic intervals. Write the interval number between your counterpoint and the cantus firmus.
6. Circle all numbers representing dissonances (2, 4, 7, 9, and d5). Make sure each dissonance appears as one of the allowable dissonance types for third species counterpoint (accented and unaccented passing tones, upper and lower neighboring tones, and the nota cambiata).

Cantus firmus 1a

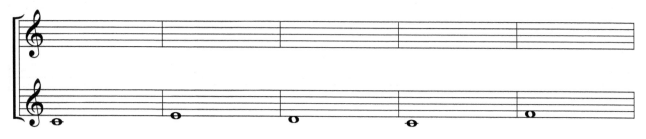

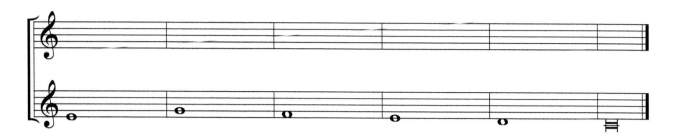

Cantus firmus 1b

Cantus firmus 2a

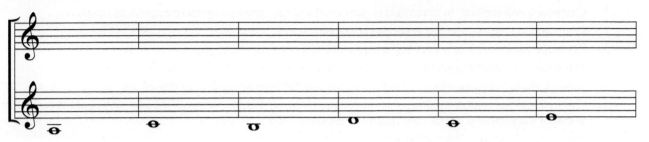

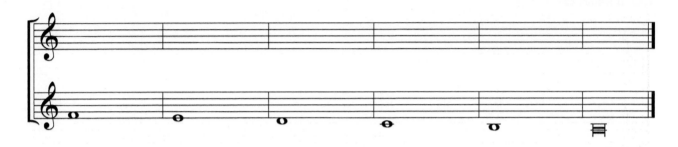

Cantus firmus 2b

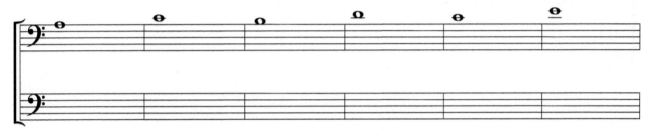

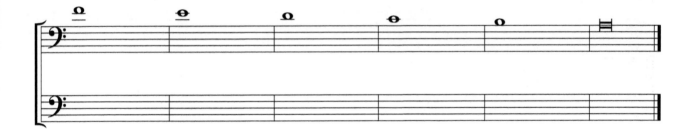

D. Following are two cantus firmus melodies.

1. Compose a counterpoint in fourth species above each cantus firmus using the principles in Chapter 8.

2. Compose a counterpoint in fourth species below each cantus firmus using the principles in Chapter 8.

3. Pay particular attention to proper beginnings and endings, as shown on page 178 of the text.

4. Make sure your counterpoint observes all the principles on pages 178–179 of the text.

5. Analyze the harmonic intervals. Write the interval number between your counterpoint and the cantus firmus.

6. Circle all numbers representing dissonances (only 2, 4, and 7 in fourth species). Make sure each dissonance appears as one of the allowable suspension types (2–3, 4–3, and 7–6).

Cantus firmus 1a

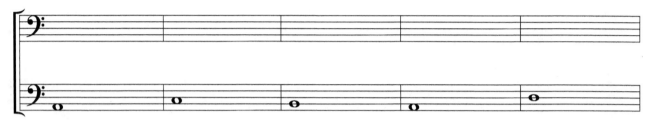

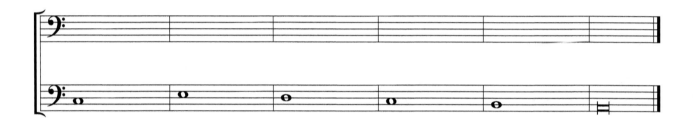

Cantus firmus 1b

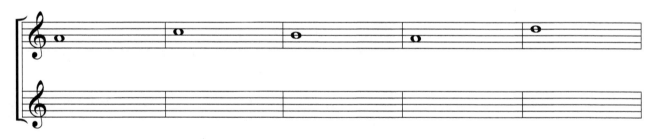

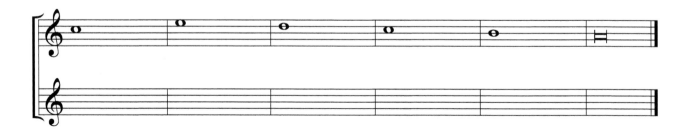

Cantus firmus 2a

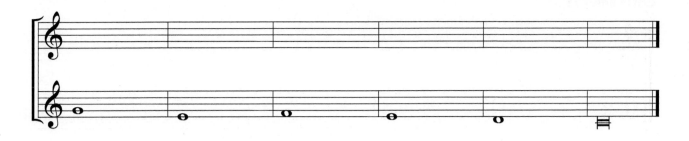

Cantus firmus 2b

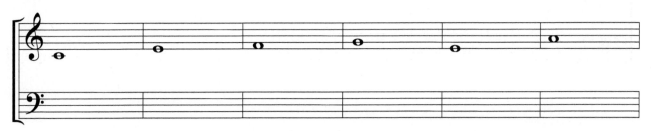

E. Following are two cantus firmus melodies.
1. Compose a counterpoint in fifth species above each cantus firmus using the principles in Chapter 8.
2. Compose a counterpoint in fifth species below each cantus firmus using the principles in Chapter 8.
3. Pay particular attention to proper beginnings and endings, as described on pages 179–180 of the text.
4. Make sure your counterpoint observes all the principles on pages 180–181 of the text.
5. Analyze the harmonic intervals. Write the interval number between your counterpoint and the cantus firmus.
6. Circle all numbers representing dissonances (2, 4, 7, 9, and d5). Make sure each dissonance appears as one of the allowable dissonance types for fifth species counterpoint.

Cantus firmus 1a

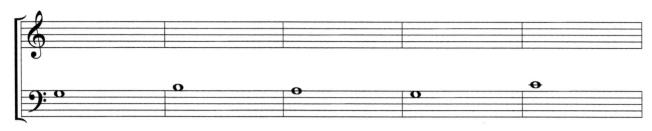

Cantus firmus 1b

Cantus firmus 2a

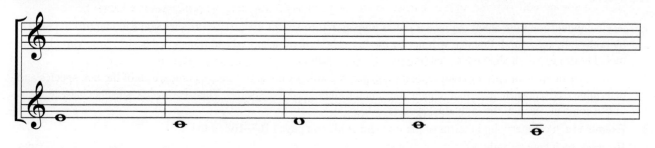

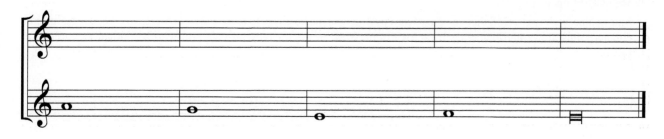

Cantus firmus 2b

Review

1. Review the information about the modal scales on pages 166–167 of the text. Make sure you can identify the modes by both sight and sound. Practice writing the modes as both nontransposed and transposed scales. Sing and play the modal scales to gain a clear understanding of how they sound.

2. Study the examples of species counterpoint on pages 163–165 of the text. Make a comparison of the five species and determine the basic principles that remain constant throughout all five species. Then, review the special characteristics that accompany each of the individual species.

3. Examine each counterpoint in terms of the melodic guides on pages 167–168 of the text.

4. Examine each counterpoint, keeping in mind the guides applicable to the relationships between two voices on pages 168–181 of the text.

5. Since voice leading is a skill that you must learn by practice, the best way to review this chapter is to compose additional counterpoints above and below each cantus firmus. Your instructor may provide you with additional examples for practice.

Test Yourself 8

Answers are on page 239.

1. Name the nine harmonic intervals allowed between the two voices in first species counterpoint.

   a. _____   b. _____   c. _____   d. _____   e. _____   f. _____   g. _____

   h. _____   i. _____

2. Name the only dissonance type allowed in second species counterpoint. _____

3. Name the five dissonance types allowed in third species counterpoint.

   a. _____   b. _____   c. _____

   d. _____   e. _____

4. Name the three types of suspensions that can be included in fourth species counterpoint.

   a. _____   b. _____   c. _____

5. Name the three modes that include the addition of musica ficta at the end of the counterpoint.

   a. _____   b. _____   c. _____

6. In the example below, there are several violations of the principles of fifth species counterpoint. Analyze the intervals between the cantus firmus and the counterpoint. Note all violations of good voice-leading practice.

CHAPTER 9
Voice Leading in Four-Part Chorale Writing

A. Following are five harmonized chorale phrases. Each phrase contains errors in part writing. On a separate sheet of paper, list the errors in each phrase. The chords are numbered for easy identification.

To refresh your memory, here are a number of common errors in four-voice writing.

1. Parallel 5ths, octaves, and unisons are to be avoided.
2. Never double the leading tone of the scale.
3. Keep each of the four voices within its range.
4. Avoid the augmented 2nd and the augmented 4th in the melodic line of any of the four voices.
5. The root should be doubled when a triad is in root position (first choice).
6. The soprano voice should be doubled when major or minor triads are in first inversion (first choice).
7. The bass note should be doubled when diminished triads are in first inversion. Root position diminished triads are seldom found.
8. All factors of triads should be present.
9. Avoid large leaps of a 6th or more. Octave leaps are an exception.
10. Maintain an octave or less between soprano and alto and between alto and tenor voices.

1. "Jesu, meine Zuversicht" ("Jesus, My Sure Defense").

2. "Als Jesus Christus in der Nacht" ("As Jesus was Betrayed in the Night").

3. "Christ lag in Todesbanden" ("Christ Lay in the Bonds of Death").

4. "Komm, Gott Schöpfer, heiliger Geist" ("Come God, Creator, Holy Ghost").

5. "Christus, der uns selig macht" ("Christ Who Makes Us Holy").

B. Each of the following exercises consists of a single progression.
1. Add the alto and tenor voices to these progressions.
2. Observe traditional part-writing practices as enumerated in the text.
3. In the blanks below the staves, provide a complete harmonic analysis of each chord.

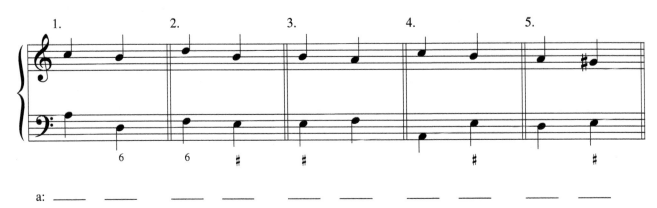

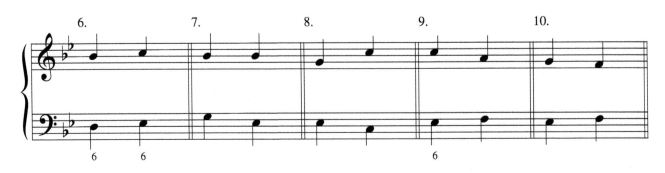

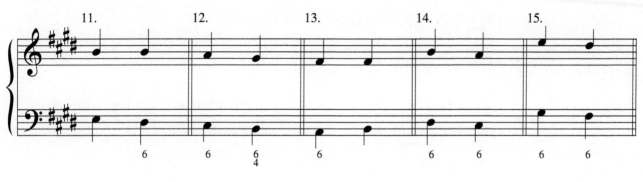

E: ___ ___ ___ ___ ___ ___ ___ ___ ___ ___

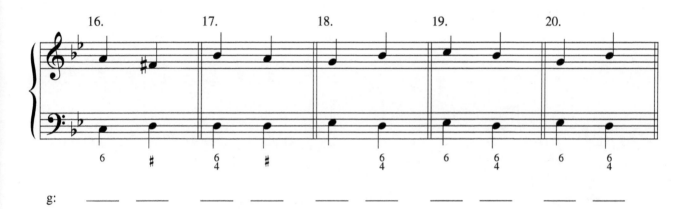

g: ___ ___ ___ ___ ___ ___ ___ ___ ___ ___

C. Below are six harmonized chorale phrases.
1. Analyze each chord using Roman numerals and indications for inversions.
2. Circle all nonharmonic tones and indicate the type by using the abbreviations in the list that follows.
3. Name the cadence type that concludes each phrase.

Nonharmonic Tones

PT = Unaccented passing tone

$\overset{>}{PT}$ = Accented passing tone

NT = Neighboring tone

7–6 SUS = 7–6 suspension

4–3 SUS = 4–3 suspension

___: ___ ___ ___ ___ ___ ___   ___: ___ ___ ___ ___ ___ ___
Key   Key

_____   _____
Cadence   Cadence

3.

Key _____ : __ __ __ __ __ __ __ __ __

Cadence _____

4.

Key _____ : __ __ __ __ __ __ __ __ __

Cadence _____

5.

Key _____ : __ __ __ __ __ __ __ __ __

Cadence _____

6.

Key _____ : __ __ __ __ __ __ __ __ __

Cadence _____

D. Following are eight chorale phrases that have been harmonized by Bach.

1. Make a complete harmonic analysis of each phrase, including Roman numerals and indications for inversions.

2. Circle each nonharmonic tone and, using the abbreviations listed below, indicate its type.

> PT = Unaccented passing tone
>
> $\overset{>}{PT}$ = Accented passing tone
>
> NT = Neighboring tone
>
> 9–8 SUS = 9–8 suspension
>
> 4–3 SUS = 4–3 suspension

1. "Wie schön leuchtet der Morgenstern" ("How Brightly Shines the Morning Star"), BWV 172, mm. 1–2.

2. "Ermuntre dich, mein schwacher Geist" ("Rouse Thyself, My Weak Spirit"), BWV 43, mm. 5–8.

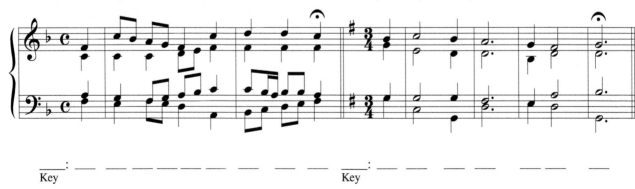

Key _____ : __ __ __ __ __ __ __ __ __

Key _____ : __ __ __ __ __ __ __ __ __

3. "Alle Menschen müssen sterben" ("All Men Must Die"), BWV 262, mm. 1–2.

4. "Wer weiss, wie nahe mir mein Ende" ("Who Knows How Near My End May Be"), BWV 166, mm. 1–3.

Key_____ : _____ _____ _____ _____ _____ _____

Key_____ : _____ _____ _____ _____ _____ _____

5. "Es ist gewisslich an der Zeit" ("It is Certainly Time"), BWV 307, mm. 1–2.

6. "Wer nur den lieben Gott lässt walten" ("He Who Lets Only Beloved God Rule"), BWV 197, mm. 1–3.

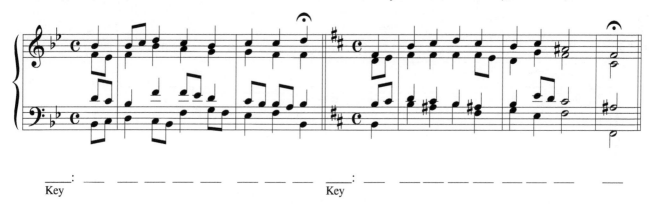

Key_____ : _____ _____ _____ _____ _____ _____

Key_____ : _____ _____ _____ _____ _____ _____

7. "Vater unser im Himmelreich" ("Our Father, Who Art in Heaven"), BWV 102, mm. 1–2.

8. "Herzlich lieb hab' ich dich, o Herr" ("I Love Thee Dearly, O Lord"), BWV 340, mm. 1–2.

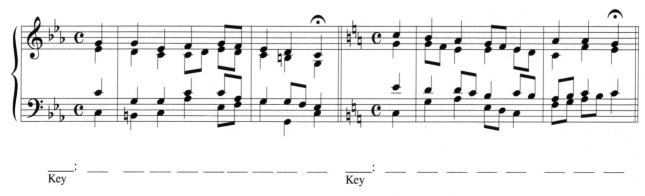

Key_____ : _____ _____ _____ _____ _____ _____

Key_____ : _____ _____ _____ _____ _____ _____

E. Each exercise consists of a chorale phrase.
 1. Add the alto and tenor voices according to the figured-bass symbols. The numbers appearing mid staff in several of the exercises refer to the voice-leading explanations listed at the bottom of the page.
 2. Observe traditional part-writing practices as given in the text.
 3. In the blanks below the staves, provide a complete harmonic analysis of each chord.

1.

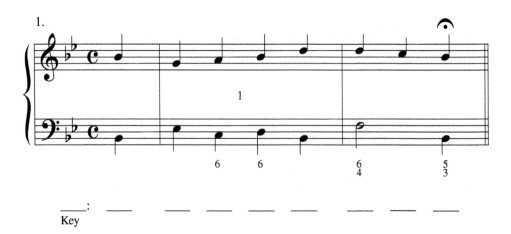

2.

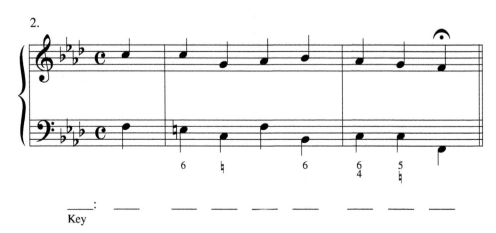

3.

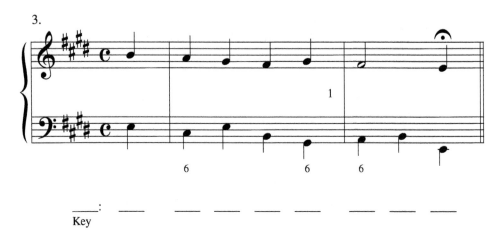

1. Alternate soprano and bass doubling in successive triads in first inversion.

4.

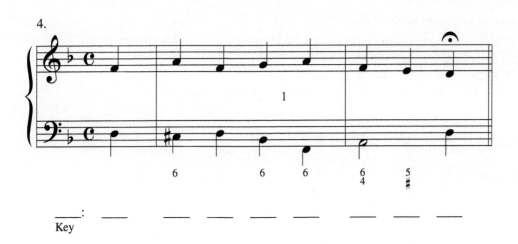

_____: __ __ __ __ __ __ __
Key

5.

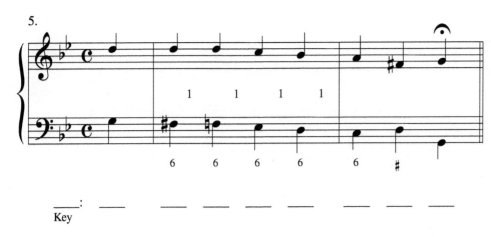

_____: __ __ __ __ __ __ __
Key

6.

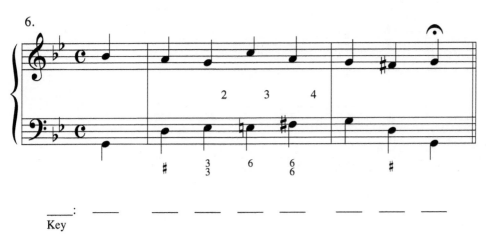

_____: __ __ __ __ __ __ __
Key

2. Double the 3rd of the VI triad to avoid augmented 2nd in alto voice. The vi and VI triads almost always receive this treatment when preceded by V.

3. The E-natural is a result of the melodic minor scale.

4. Double the 6th above bass note here. Doubling the soprano will create parallel octaves, and doubling the bass note doubles the leading tone of the scale.

7.

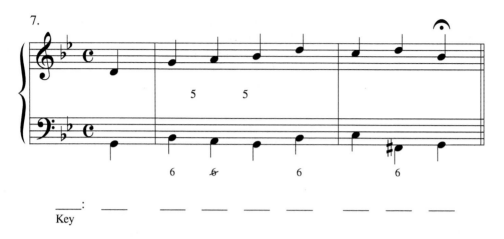

Key

8.

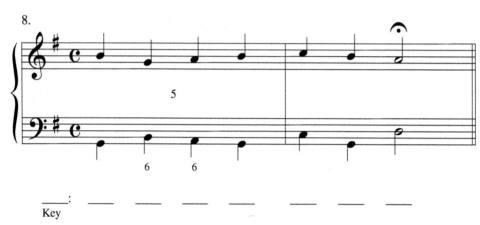

Key

9.

Key

5.   Investigate the possibility of unequal 5ths here (perfect to diminished or vice versa). Are alternatives possible?

F. Following is an excerpt from a *trio sonata,* one of the most important types of composition in the baroque period. A trio sonata consists of two upper parts (usually taken by violins, flutes, and so on) and a lower part that includes a figured bass. A gambist (performer on the viola da gamba) or cellist plays the lower line while a harpsichordist or pianist *realizes* the continuo part (plays the chords requested by the figured bass).

Write out the tenor and alto parts of the continuo according to the figured-bass symbols. Observe traditional part-writing procedures as indicated in the text.

Vivaldi: *Sonata da camera a tre* (Chamber Sonata for Three) in D Minor.

G. Following is a chorale melody with figured bass.

1. Add alto and tenor voices according to the figured-bass symbols.

2. Unless voice leading dictates otherwise, make your part writing conform to recommended practices.

3. Add nonharmonic tones wherever appropriate.

4. Play your harmonization in class.

The following hints will help you complete this realization:

a. The E♭ circled in the bass voice of measure 7 is a passing tone. Disregard it when completing the chord.

b. In measure 8, the figures 4 and 3 indicate that you should add a 4–3 suspension.

c. Although most of this harmonization can be completed following the recommended stylistic practices, you may find it necessary to adjust your voice leading in measures 7 and 13 to accommodate the given elements. Consider voice overlap or secondary recommendations for doublings in these measures.

d. A key signature of one flat typically suggests F major or D minor, but this composition is not in either of these two keys. Can you identify the key of this composition? (Hint: consider the recurring accidentals given in the figured bass.)

"Herzliebster Jesu, was hast du verbrochen" from the *Nuremberg Songbook*, 1677.

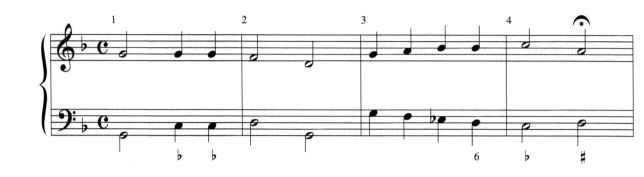

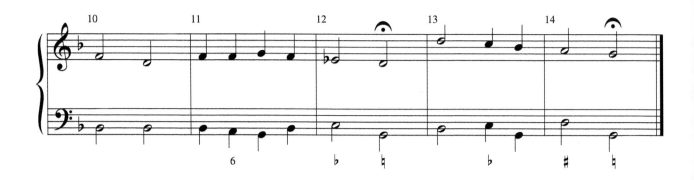

H. Refer to "Danket dem Herren, denn er ist sehr freundlich" by Bach on page 169.

   1. Provide a Roman numeral for each chord and specify inverions.

   2. Circle all nonharmonic tones and write the abbreviations representing the name nearby.

   3. Examine the voice-leading throughout the chorale and identify the stylistic practices used to move from one chord to the next. (The stylistic practices are presented in Chapter 9 on pages 194–201 of the text and summarized in Appendix A on page 373.) Identify any exceptions to standard voice-leading practice.

I. Refer to Handel's "Hallelujah!" from the *Messiah* on page 198.

   Examine measures 4–10. Identify any exceptions to standard voice-leading practice as stated in Chapter 9. Describe any exceptions below.

   _____

   _____

   _____

   _____

J. The following chorales, harmonized by Bach, can be used for further study of voice-leading practices:

   "O Herre Gott, dein göttlich Wort" (page 173)

   "Gottes Sohn ist kommen" (page 170)

   "Christus, der ist mein Leben" (page 169)

   "O Ewigkeit, du Donnerwort" (page 172)

   "Straf' mich nicht in deinem Zorn" (page 174)

   "Jesu, du mein liebstes Leben" (page 171)

   "Werde munter, mein Gemüte" (page 175)

Review

The techniques of voice leading allow you to connect chords smoothly, creating parts that are easily singable. These techniques will not, in themselves, allow you to produce interesting music, but they are important standard procedures that you will use many times in future chapters, so it is important that they be thoroughly mastered.

1. Review the voice-leading principles for two-voice species counterpoint in Chapter 8. Continue to write species counterpoints above and below each cantus firmus in the text and workbook. Most of the basic principles of voice leading in four voices come from species counterpoint.

2. Examine the soprano melodies of several of the Bach chorales on pages 169–175 in the Anthology in relationship with the bass voices. Notice how the principles of species counterpoint are observed in these two-voice combinations.

3. Study the principles of four-voice writing on text pages 194–201 and the common errors shown on pages 202–203. These guidelines will enable you to create smooth four-voice voice leading.

4. Since voice leading is a technique that can only be learned by practice, use figured basses that have not been assigned by your instructor for extra practice.

Test Yourself 9

Answers are on pages 239–240.

1. Below is a four-voice chorale phrase that contains a number of errors in voice leading. Place Roman numerals in the blanks provided and describe the errors you see in the phrase.

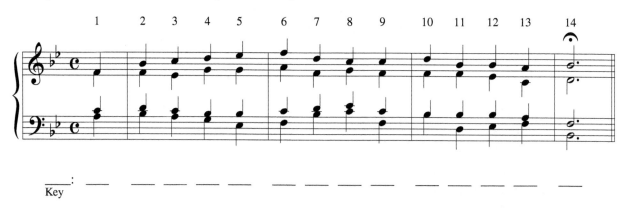

2. Complete the second chord in each of the excerpts below. The key in each case is C major. Place Roman numerals in the blanks provided. Observe the figured-bass symbols and pay particular attention to the chord qualities involved.

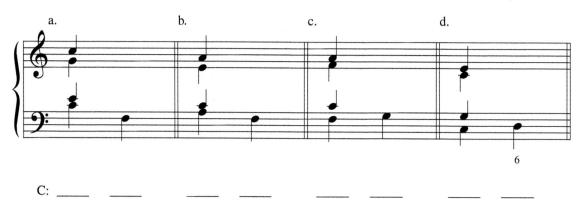

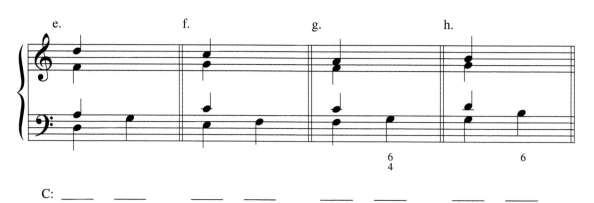

CHAPTER 10
Harmonic Progression and Harmonic Rhythm

A. Following are eight harmonized chorale phrases.

1. Analyze each chord using Roman numerals and indications for inversions.
2. Circle all nonharmonic tones and indicate the type by using the abbreviations in the following list.
3. Name the cadence type that concludes each phrase.

Nonharmonic Tones

PT = Unaccented passing tone
$\overset{>}{PT}$ = Accented passing tone
NT = Neighboring tone
7–6 SUS = 7–6 suspension
4–3 SUS = 4–3 suspension
ET = Escape tone
ANT = Anticipation
APP = Appoggiatura

B. Following are five short excerpts in keyboard style.
1. Bracket the harmonic rhythm.
2. Analyze each harmonic area using Roman numerals and indications for inversions.
3. Circle and identify any nonharmonic tones.
4. Name the cadence type that concludes each phrase.

1. Scarlatti: Sonata in G Major, K. 391, L. 79, mm. 1–4.

2. Anonymous: Menuet in G Major from the *Notebook for Anna Magdalena Bach*, mm. 1–8.

3. Purcell: Prelude from Suite in G Major.

4. Handel: Passacaille from Suite in G Minor, G. 255, mm. 9–16.

5. Bach: Little Prelude in F Major, BWV 927, mm. 1–5.

C. Following are seven chorale melodies with figured bass.

1. Add alto and tenor voices according to the figured-bass symbols.
2. Unless voice leading dictates otherwise, make your part writing conform to recommended practices.
3. Analyze each chord—blanks are provided.
4. Add nonharmonic tones wherever appropriate.
5. Play your harmonization in class.

1. "Herr Jesu Christ, du höchstes Gut" ("Lord Jesus Christ, Thou Highest Good").

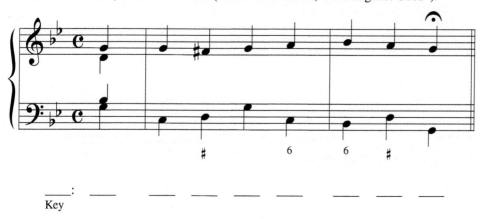

____: __ __ __ __ __ __ __ __
Key

2. "Der Tag, der ist so freudenreich" ("This Day is so Joyful").

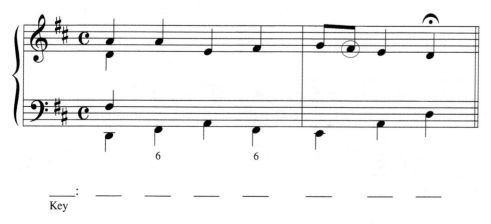

____: __ __ __ __ __ __ __ __
Key

3. "Meinen Jesum lass' ich nicht" ("I Will Not Leave My Jesus").

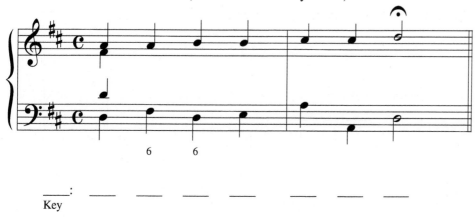

____: __ __ __ __ __ __ __ __
Key

4. "Von Himmel hoch du komm' ich her" ("From Heaven Above I Come").

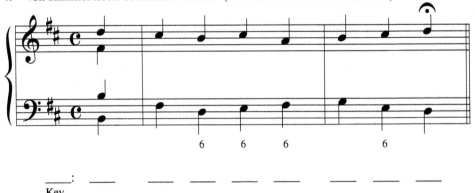

_____: __ __ __ __ __
Key

5. "Du Friedensfürst, Herr Jesu Christ" ("Thou Prince of Peace, Lord Jesus Christ").

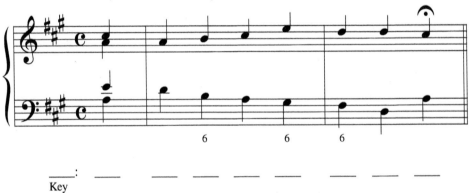

_____: __ __ __ __ __
Key

6. "Vater unser im Himmelreich" ("Our Father Who Art in Heaven").

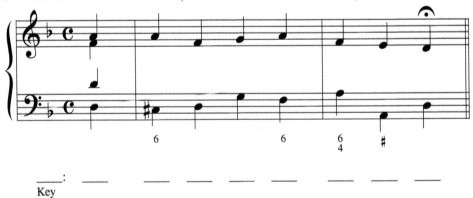

_____: __ __ __ __ __ __
Key

7. "Wach' auf, mein Herz, und singe" ("Awake, My Heart, and Sing").

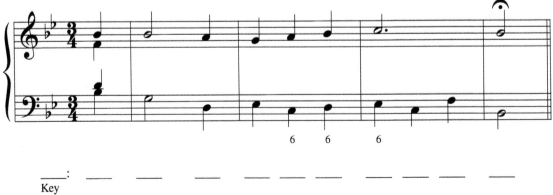

_____: __ __ __ __ __
Key

D. Each exercise represents a figured-bass voice.
   1. Complete the remaining three upper voices (soprano, alto, and tenor) according to the figuration supplied.
   2. Try to make each voice as interesting as possible, but the soprano should have priority. You will achieve maximum success by writing the entire soprano voice first, then filling in the alto and tenor as needed.
   3. Be sure to observe part-writing practices as cited in the text.
   4. Provide a complete Roman numeral analysis of each completed figured bass. Blanks are provided.

1.

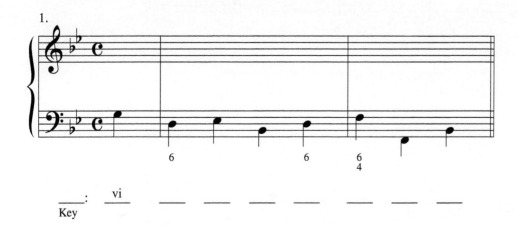

2.

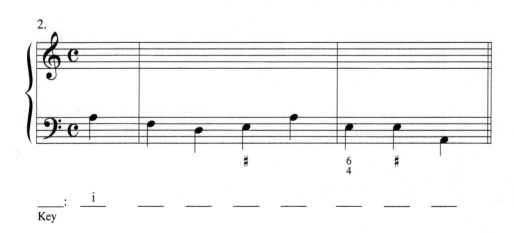

3.

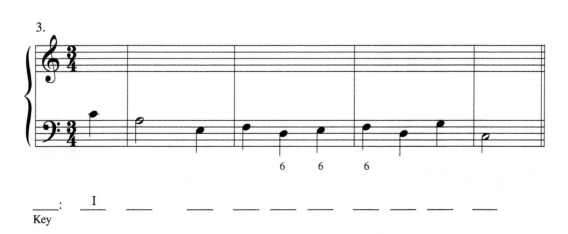

E. Following are excerpts from six string quartets by Mozart.

1. On a separate piece of paper, determine the harmonic rhythm—the number and placement of the triads.

2. In a column under each change of harmony, write the letter names (designating the roots) or chord symbols for all possible triads that could be used to harmonize the melody.

3. Indicate the obvious nonharmonic tones. These need not agree with the basic triads you select.

4. Select the cadence chords.

5. Draw a line between all adjacent chords whose roots form a descending P5th progression.

6. Chart three or four possible harmonizations using a majority of ascending P4th progressions, separating such series with a descending 3rd or an ascending 2nd progression.

7. Sing or play the melody and accompany it on the piano with each of your proposed harmonic selections.

8. Experiment with different harmonic rhythms, using some containing frequent chord changes and others with very few.

9. Play at least one of each student's harmonizations in class and have the class members determine which they find most appropriate.

10. Arrange some of the harmonizations for string quartet, woodwind quartet, brass quartet, piano, harpsichord, or any other medium available to the class.

1. Mozart: String Quartet in G Major, K. 80, III: Trio, mm. 1–8.

2. Mozart: String Quartet in G Major, K. 80, IV: Rondeau, mm. 1–8.

3. Mozart: String Quartet in G Major, K. 156, III: Tempo di Menuetto, mm. 1–8.

4. Mozart: String Quartet in B-flat Major, K. 159, III: Rondo, mm. 1–8.

5. Mozart: String Quartet in C Major, K. 157, III: Presto, mm. 1–8.

6. Mozart: String Quartet in C Major, K. 157, I: Allegro, mm. 1–8.

F. Refer to "Ich schell mein Horn ins Jammertal," op. 43, no. 3, by Johannes Brahms (1833–1897) on page 185.
   1. Have a member of the class play the accompaniment while the rest of the class sings the vocal line.
   2. Determine the harmonic rhythm.
   3. Analyze each chord using macro analysis symbols:

      Major = Capital letter
      Minor = Lowercase letter
      Diminished = Lowercase letter plus °
      Augmented = Capital letter plus ⁺

   4. Add the macro analysis slur symbol between all circle progressions (progressions with root movement of a descending 5th or an ascending 4th).
   5. Prepare a chart indicating the number of:
      a. Descending 5th (ascending 4th) progressions.
      b. Ascending 5th (descending 4th) progressions.
      c. Ascending 2nd (descending 7th) progressions.
      d. Descending 3rd (ascending 6th) progressions.
      e. Ascending 3rd (descending 6th) progressions.
      f. Descending 2nd (ascending 7th) progressions.

G. Refer to "The New Sa-Hoo" from the *Fitzwilliam Virginal Book* by Giles Farnaby (ca. 1560–1640) on page 194.
   1. Bracket the harmonic rhythm.
   2. Analyze each harmonic area using Roman numerals and indications for inversions.
   3. Circle all nonharmonic tones and write the abbreviations representing the name nearby.
   4. Name the cadence type that concludes each phrase.

H. Following are several folk songs.

1. First, determine the harmonic rhythm—the number and placement of the triads—for each.

2. In a column under each change of harmony, write the letter names (designating the roots) or chord symbols for all possible triads that could be used to harmonize the melody.

3. Indicate the obvious nonharmonic tones. These need not agree with the basic triads you select.

4. Select the cadence chords.

5. Draw a line between all adjacent chords whose roots form a descending P5th (ascending P4th) progression.

6. Chart three or four possible harmonizations, using a majority of descending P5th progressions while separating such series with descending 3rd or ascending 2nd progressions.

7. Sing or play the melody and accompany it on the piano with each of your proposed harmonic selections.

8. Experiment with different harmonic rhythms, using some containing frequent chord changes and some with very few.

9. Play at least one of each student's harmonizations in class and have the class members determine which they find most appropriate.

10. Arrange some of the harmonizations for guitar, piano, instrumental ensembles, or any other medium available to the class.

1. Welsh Folk Song: "Ash Grove."

2. Irish Folk Song: "Cockles and Mussels."

3. Scottish Folk Song: "The Wearing of the Green."

4. German Song: "Our Thoughts, They Are Free."

5. French Song: "Au Clair de Lune."

6. Minstrel Song: "Jimmy Crack Corn."

7. American Work Song: "I've Been Working on the Railroad."

8. Norwegian Folk Song: "Behold a Host."

Review

The technique of melody harmonization is at the heart of this chapter. The central importance of the circle of 5th progression (circle progression) in achieving a satisfactory harmonization cannot be overemphasized.

1. Choose a few pieces from a collection of traditional and patriotic songs, a hymnal, or some similar music. Name the root of each chord. (You may not be able to do a Roman numeral analysis of the entire piece because the chord vocabulary may not have been covered yet.) Mark each example of a circle progression you discover. Try to find examples of several circle progressions in succession. How often do these progressions reach the tonic chord as a target?

2. Review the sections on the vii° and the second inversion tonic triad on pages 217–218 of the text. Remember that the leading-tone triad is closely related to the dominant and counts as a weaker circle progression when it progresses to the tonic chord. The tonic triad in second inversion is usually a decoration of the dominant chord that follows immediately.

3. Practice harmonizing chorale melodies, using examples from the assignments or familiar hymn tunes. Try to use as many circle progressions as possible in your harmonizations. Remember that each phrase must end with one of the standard cadences.

4. This would be a good time to review the materials of Chapters 5 and 9; you will need to have them clearly in mind as you work on your chorale harmonizations. Music theory is a cumulative subject, and you must constantly review previous materials to keep them fresh in your mind.

Test Yourself 10

Answers are on page 240.

Below are several phrases from a chorale setting by Otto Nicolai (1810–49) with each pair of chords identified by a number.

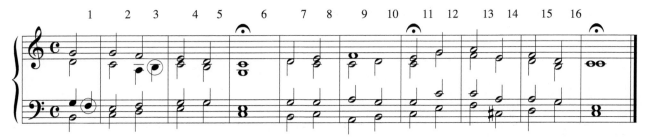

1. List all the progressions according to type, as follows:
   a. Circle progressions
   b. Descending 3rd progressions
   c. Ascending 2nd progressions
   d. Other progressions
2. What conclusion could you reach by studying the tabulation of progression types in question 1?

On the next page is a chorale melody with possible chords for a harmonization (only one choice is given for the first note of the melody and the final note of each phrase).

"O Ewigkeit, du Donnerwort" ("Oh Eternity, Thou Word of Thunder"), mm. 1–6.

I	iii	IV	V	V	vi	vii°	I	I	iii	IV	V	V
I	ii	iii	iii	IV	V		vi	I	ii	iii	iii	
vi	vii°	I	I	ii	iii		IV	vi	vii°	I	I	

IV	iii	V	iii	I	I	IV	iii	ii	ii	I
ii	I		I	vi	vi	ii	I	vii°	vii°	
vii°	vi		vi	IV	IV	vii°	vi	V	V	

3. Mark all possible circle progressions with a line between the Roman numerals. Choose a single chord for each quarter note that takes advantage of the maximum number of circle progressions. If no circle progression is possible try to choose an ascending 2nd or descending 3rd progression. You should have at least twelve circle progressions in your harmonization.

4. Compare your chord choices with the setting of this chorale by Bach on page 172. (Bach's setting uses 7th chords and some chromatic harmony that you have not studied as yet.) How often does your chord choice agree with that of Bach?

CHAPTER 11
The Dominant Seventh Chord

A. Write a major-minor 7th chord above each of the given tones. The example illustrates the correct procedure.

B. Each of the following chords is a dominant (major-minor) 7th.
   1. Provide a circle resolution for each chord.
   2. Analyze both chords—the chord succeeding the dominant 7th will be the tonic triad of a major key.
   The example illustrates the correct procedure.

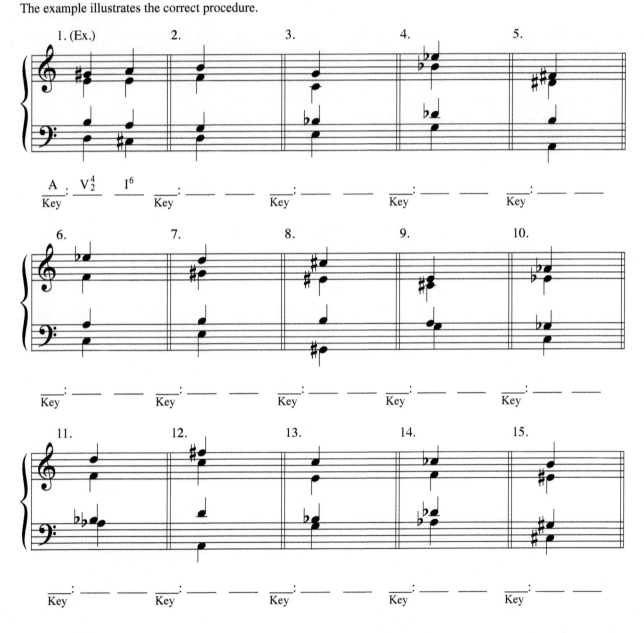

C. Following are eight harmonized chorales containing dominant 7th chords.

1. Analyze each chord. Blanks are provided.

2. Name the cadence type that concludes each phrase.

3. Circle all nonharmonic tones and indicate the type by using the abbreviations in the following list.

Nonharmonic Tones

PT = Unaccented passing tone

$\overset{>}{PT}$ = Accented passing tone

NT = Neighboring tone

7–6 SUS = 7–6 suspension

4–3 SUS = 4–3 suspension

ET = Escape tone

ANT = Anticipation

APP = Appoggiatura

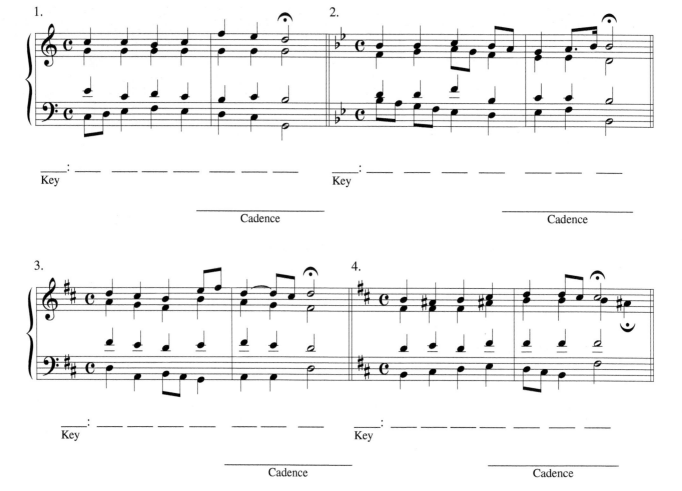

5.

Key ___ : __ __ __ __ __ __ __ __

Cadence _____

6.

Key ___ : __ __ __ __ __ __ __ __

Cadence _____

7.

Key ___ : __ __ __ __ __ __ __ __

Cadence _____

8.

Key ___ : __ __ __ __ __ __ __ __

Cadence _____

D. Following are four excerpts from music literature that include dominant 7th chords.

1. Analyze each chord using Roman numerals and indications for inversions.

2. Circle and identify any nonharmonic tones.

3. Name the cadence type that concludes each phrase.

1. Corelli: Sarabande in D Minor, mm. 1–8.

2. Mozart: Sonata in G Major, K. 283, I, mm. 1–10.

3. Brahms: Romance from Six Piano Pieces, op. 118, no. 5, mm. 1–5.

4. Beethoven: Rondo in C Major, op. 51, no. 1, mm. 1–17.

E. Following are seven chorale melodies with figured bass.
1. Add alto and tenor voices according to the figured-bass symbols.
2. Make sure your part writing conforms to recommended practice.
3. Analyze each chord—blanks are provided.
4. Add chord tones and nonharmonic tones (usually eighth notes) to improve voice leading.
5. Play your harmonization in class.

1. "Schmücke dich o liebe Seele" ("Prepare Thyself, Dear Soul").

2. "Wenn wir in höchsten Nöten sein" ("When We Are in Utmost Need").

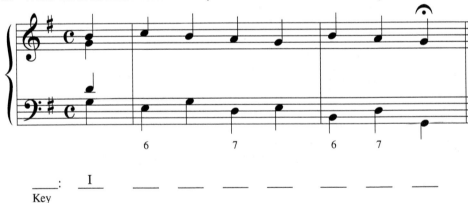

3. "Jesu, Jesu, du bist mein" ("Jesus, Jesus, Thou Art Mine").

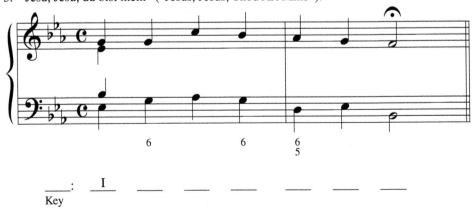

4. "Ich freue mich in dir" ("I Rejoice in Thee").

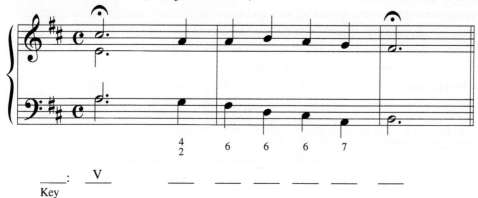

$\begin{array}{cccc} 4 & 6 & 6 & 6 & 7 \\ 2 \end{array}$

____: V
Key

5. "Auf, auf, mein Herz, mit Freuden" ("Up, Up, My Heart, with Joy") .

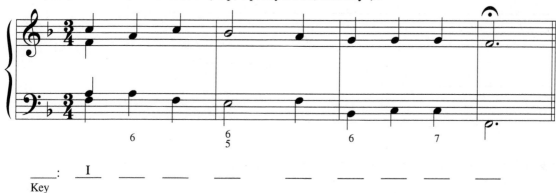

6   6   6   7
     5

____: I
Key

6. "Erwürgtes Lamm" ("Slaughtered Lamb").

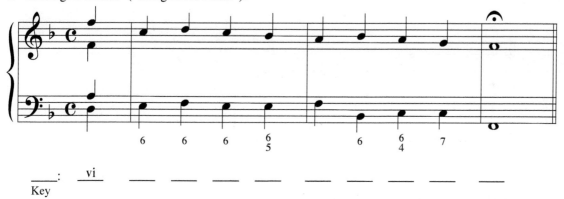

6   6   6   6   6   6   7
            5   4

____: vi
Key

7. "Mein Jesu, dem die Seraphinen" ("My Jesus, Whom the Seraphim").

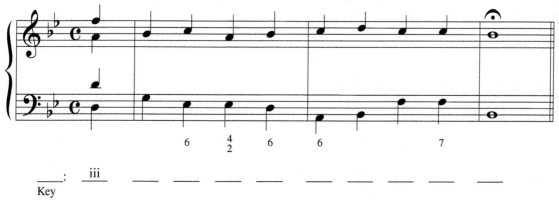

6   4   6   6   7
    2

____: iii
Key

F. Each exercise represents a figured-bass voice.
1. Complete the remaining three upper voices (soprano, alto, and tenor) according to the figuration supplied.
2. Try to make each voice as interesting as possible, but the soprano should have priority. You will have best results by writing the entire soprano voice first, then filling in the alto and tenor as needed.
3. Be sure to observe voice-leading practices as cited in the text.
4. Provide a complete Roman numeral analysis of each completed figured bass. Blanks are provided.

1.

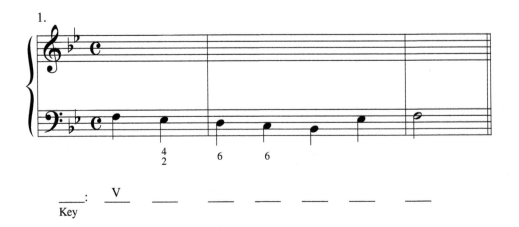

2.

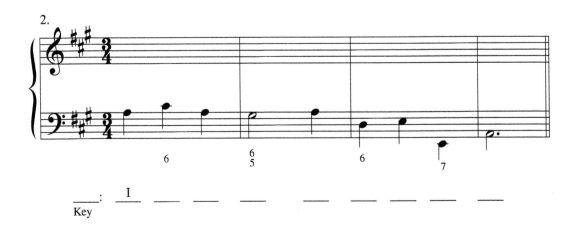

3.

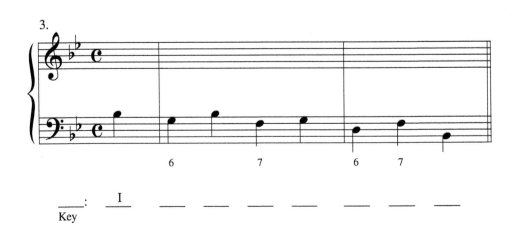

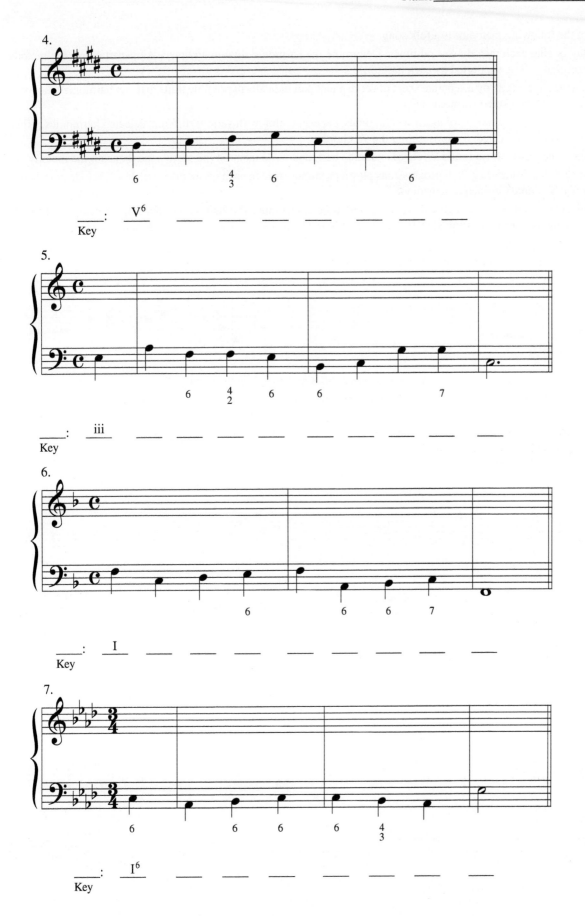

G. Each of the following melodies is a folk song.

1. Play or sing each melody several times. Determine the harmonic rhythm and place a bracket above the melody tones that will be supported by each harmony.

2. Rewrite the melody on a separate sheet of score paper and indicate all possible traits that can harmonize the tones within each bracketed harmonic area.

3. Play or sing the melody over again several times, experimenting with various different selected harmonies. When the V triad is indicated, try substituting the V^7 chord.

4. Select the series of triads and V^7 chords you like best, and write them on the score paper beneath the melody.

5. Be sure that descending P5th progressions play a prominent role in each harmonization. Also, include at least one or two V^7 chords in each arrangement.

6. Select an accompaniment figure that can be used more or less intact throughout. The accompaniment figure should fit the medium (piano, stringed instruments, woodwind instruments, brass instruments, and so on).

7. Fit the accompaniment figure to each successive chord and complete the composition.

8. Assign the melody itself to a solo voice or instrument. If you wish, make up some words of your own for the folk song melody.

9. Play some of the compositions in class. Have the students decide which harmonic rhythm and harmonization is most suitable for the particular melody.

1. American Folk Song (this particular folk song is based on a pentatonic scale).

2. Russian Folk Song.

Except for the beginning of each phrase, the following composition can be harmonized using descending P5th (ascending P4th) progressions.

3. Balkan Folk Song.

4. Russian Folk Song.

5. American Folk Song.

H. Refer to Schubert's German Dance, D. 975, on page 226.
   1. Listen to the composition to determine the harmonic rhythm.
   2. Analyze each chord using Roman numerals and indications for inversions.
   3. Circle and identify any nonharmonic tones.
   4. Name the cadence type that concludes each phrase.
   5. Study the voice leading for each dominant 7th chord. Do the dominant 7ths resolve as expected?

I.   Refer to Mozart's "Das Kinderspiel," which follows.

   1.   Have a member of the class play the composition while the sopranos sing the upper voice and the basses and baritones sing the lowest voice.

   2.   Bracket the harmonic rhythm; that is, place a bracket over the tones that fall within each harmony.

   3.   Do a Roman numeral analysis of the excerpt.

   4.   On a separate sheet of paper, indicate the type of resolution for each major-minor 7th chord (circle progression, noncircle progression with resolution, or nonresolution of the 7th factor).

   5.   Arrange this excerpt for a group of instruments played by members of the class.

Mozart: "Das Kinderspiel" ("The Children's Game"), K. 598, mm. 1–8.

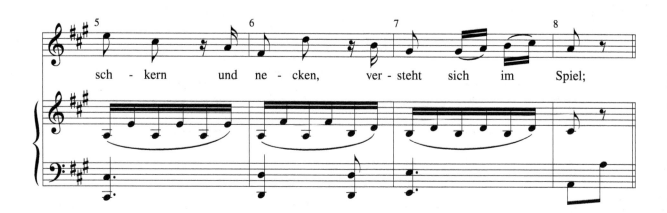

Review

1. Look at the circle of 5ths on page 38 of the text. Spell the dominant 7th chord in each major and minor key. Remember to use the harmonic form of the minor scales. Write the dominant 7th in four parts and resolve it to the tonic chord, making sure that the 7th resolves downward by step. Use the first example in Figure 11.10 on page 240 of the text as a model for your progression. Play the progressions on the piano.

2. Repeat the procedure above, resolving the dominant 7th chord to VI or vi. Use the second example in Figure 11.11 on page 241 as a model for this progression. Play this progression on the piano.

3. Remember that the list of terms at the beginning of each chapter forms a convenient list of important concepts you need to understand. See if you remember the important information about each of the listed terms. Pay particular attention to the specific figured-bass symbols for the inversions of the 7th chords.

4. Work out assignments that were not completed during your study of the chapter for practice in dealing with the dominant 7th chord.

5. Dominant 7th chords are by far the most common 7th chords in tonal music. Find examples of dominant 7ths in familiar music and see if the part-writing principles contained in this chapter are observed. Does the 7th of the chord move downward by step? If not, can you see how its resolution is accounted for in the music?

Test Yourself 11

Answers are on page 241.

Question 1 refers to this musical example:

1. Each of the chords is a dominant 7th chord. Determine the chord and its position and answer the following questions.

   a. Chord number 1 is the dominant 7th chord in _____ major. The 7th is in the _____ voice and will resolve to _____ (note name) in the tonic triad.

   b. Chord number 2 is the dominant 7th chord in _____ minor. The 7th is in the _____ voice and will resolve to _____ (note name) in the tonic triad.

   c. Chord number 3 is the dominant 7th chord in _____ major. The 7th is in the _____ voice and will resolve to _____ (note name) in the tonic triad.

   d. Chord number 4 is the dominant 7th chord in _____ minor. The 7th is in the _____ voice and will resolve to _____ (note name) in the tonic triad.

   e. Chord number 5 is the dominant 7th chord in _____ minor. The 7th is in the _____ voice and will resolve to _____ (note name) in the tonic triad.

   f. Chord number 6 is the dominant 7th chord in _____ major. The 7th is in the _____ voice and will resolve to _____ (note name) in the tonic triad.

Questions 2–5 refer to the musical examples below:

2. Dominant 7th chords appear at chord numbers _____ , _____ , _____ , and _____ .

3. At chord number _____ the 7th of the dominant does not resolve in the normal manner.

4. Nonharmonic tone review:

    a. The nonharmonic tone at chord number 1 is a(n) _____ .

    b. The nonharmonic tone at chord number 3 is a(n) _____ .

    c. The nonharmonic tone at chord number 5 is a(n) _____ .

    d. The nonharmonic tone at chord number 7 is a(n) _____ .

    e. The nonharmonic tone at chord number 10 is a(n) _____ .

    f. The nonharmonic tone at chord number 11 is a(n) _____ .

5. Cadence review:

    a. The cadence at chord number 4 is a(n) _____ cadence.

    b. The cadence at chord number 8 is a(n) _____ cadence.

    c. The cadence at chord number 12 is a(n) _____ cadence.

CHAPTER 12
The Leading-Tone Seventh Chords

A. Write the vii°⁷ chord above each root. The illustration demonstrates the correct procedure.

B. Write a vii⁷ chord above each root. The illustration demonstrates the correct procedure.

C. Each four-voice chord below is either a vii°⁷ or vii⁷ chord.
1. Resolve each vii°⁷ chord to a minor triad.
2. Resolve each vii⁷ chord to a major triad.

The resolution chord will always be the tonic triad and may be either in root position or in inversion. The illustration demonstrates correct procedure.

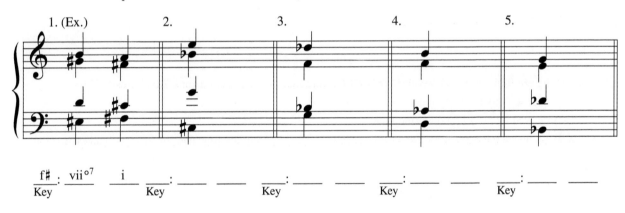

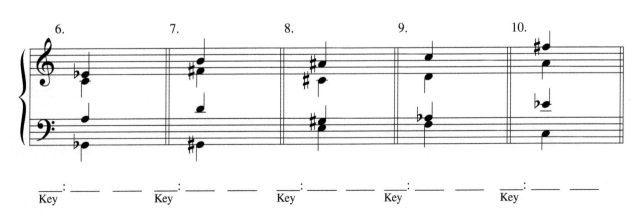

D. Each four-voice chord below is either a vii°⁷ or vii⁷ chord. Resolve each leading-tone 7th chord to the V⁷ (or inversion) before continuing to the tonic. The illustration demonstrates the correct procedure.

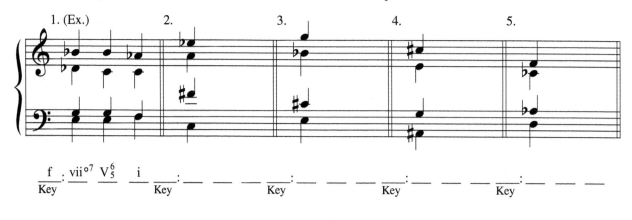

f : vii°⁷ V$_5^6$ i : _ _ _ _
Key ___ ___ ___   Key : _ _ _ _   Key : _ _ _ _   Key : _ _ _ _   Key : _ _ _ _

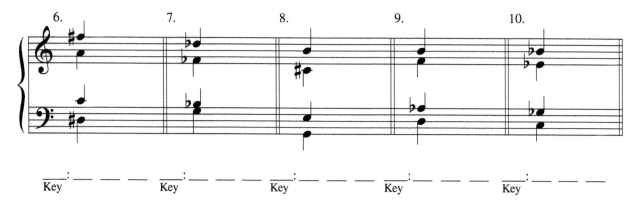

Key : _ _ _ _   Key : _ _ _ _   Key : _ _ _ _   Key : _ _ _ _   Key : _ _ _ _

E. Following are four short excerpts from music literature that include leading-tone 7th chords.
   1. Provide a Roman numeral analysis for each chord.
   2. Circle and identify all nonharmonic tones.
   3. Examine each leading-tone 7th chord and determine if the leading tone and the 7th resolve as expected.

1. Caldara: "Come raggio di sol," mm. 1–4.

Co - me rag-gio di   sol   mi - te e   se - re - no.

2. A Scarlatti: "O cessate di piagarmi" from *Pompeo*, mm. 1–4.

O ces - sa - te di pia-gar - mi, O la-scia - te - mi mo-rir,

3. Mozart: Sonata in D Major, K. 284, III: Variation V, mm. 14–17.

4. Mozart: Sonata in B-flat Major, K. 333, III: Allegretto grazioso, mm. 68–71.

CHAPTER 12   The Leading-Tone Seventh Chords   **117**

F. Each exercise below is a chorale melody with figured bass. All have been harmonized at least once by Bach.

1. Add the alto and tenor voices according to the directions provided by the figured-bass symbols.

2. A slash (e.g., $\frac{4}{3}$) means to raise that interval (above the bass note) one half step.

3. Double numbers (e.g., $\frac{8}{8}, \frac{6}{6}, \frac{3}{3}$) mean to double that interval above the bass note.

4. Analyze each chord using Roman numeral analysis.

5. Sing or play each completed harmonization in class.

1. "Das alte Jahr vergangen ist" ("The Old Year Has Passed Away").

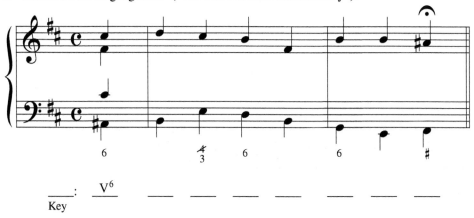

_____: V^6 ___ ___ ___ ___ ___ ___ ___
Key

2. "Ach Gott, vom Himmel sieh' darein" ("Oh God, from Heaven Look Therein").

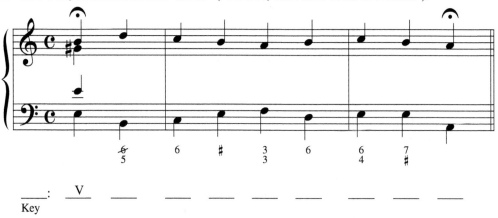

_____: V ___ ___ ___ ___ ___ ___ ___
Key

3. "Herzlich tut mich verlangen" ("I Desire Sincerely").

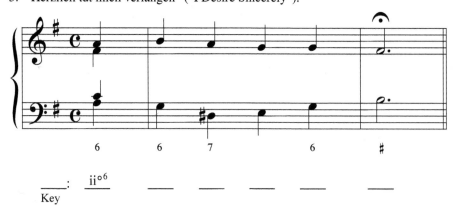

_____: $ii°^6$ ___ ___ ___ ___ ___
Key

4. "Wir Christenleut'" ("We Christian People").

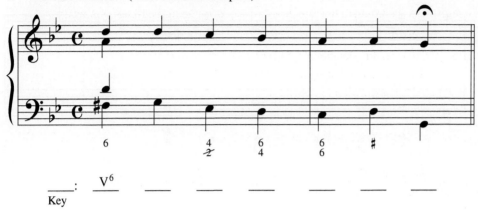

_____: V⁶   ___   ___   ___   ___   ___   ___
Key

5. "Jesu meine Freude" ("Jesus, My Joy").

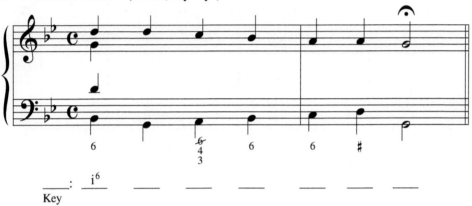

_____: i⁶   ___   ___   ___   ___   ___
Key

G. The following are additional exercises related to the exercises in F.
1. When completed, add at least four or five nonharmonic tones to each exercise.
2. Play or sing these harmonizations in class and ask class members to determine which combinations sound most appropriate.

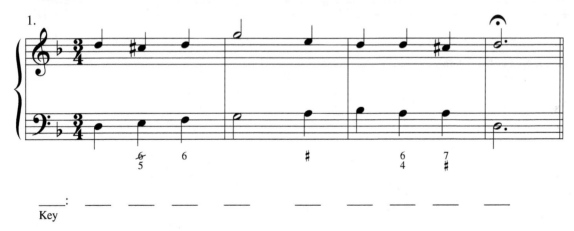

_____: ___   ___   ___   ___   ___   ___   ___
Key

2.

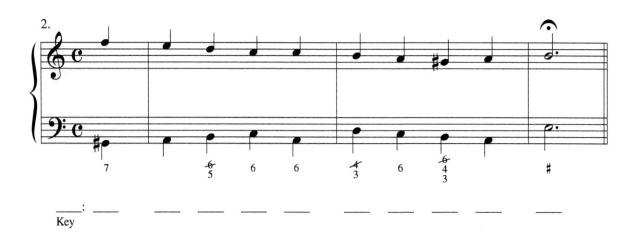

_____: __ __ __ __ __ __ __
Key

3.

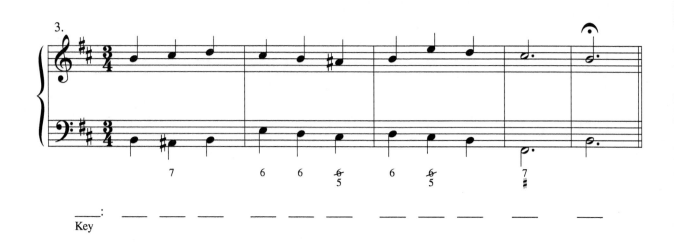

_____: __ __ __ __ __ __
Key

4.

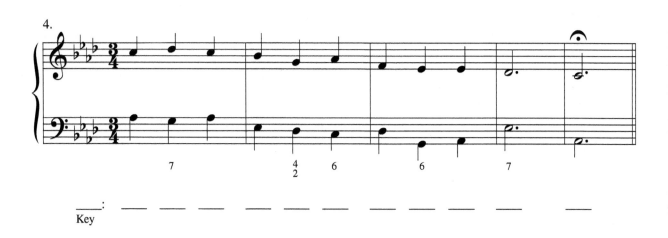

_____: __ __ __ __ __ __ __
Key

H. Each exercise represents a figured-bass voice.
   1. Complete the remaining upper voices (soprano, alto, and tenor) according to the figuration supplied.
   2. Try to make each voice as interesting as possible, but the soprano should have priority. You will have most success by writing the entire soprano voice first, then filling in the alto and tenor as needed.
   3. Be sure to observe part-writing practices as cited in the text.
   4. Provide a complete Roman numeral analysis of each completed figured bass. Blanks are provided.

1.

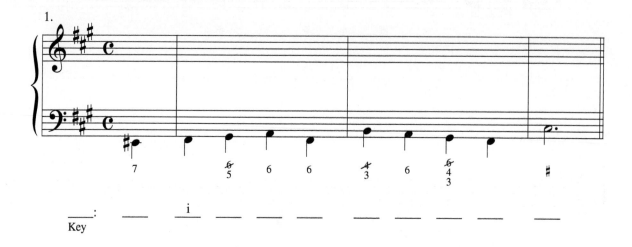

_____: ___ ___ ___ ___ ___ ___ ___ ___ ___
Key   i

2.

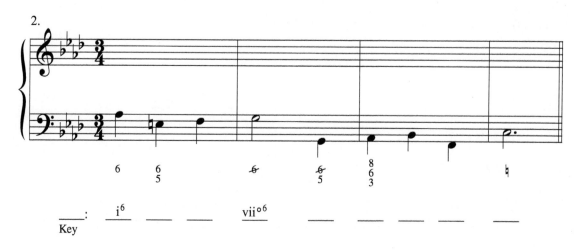

_____: i⁶ ___ ___ vii°⁶ ___ ___ ___ ___ ___
Key

3.

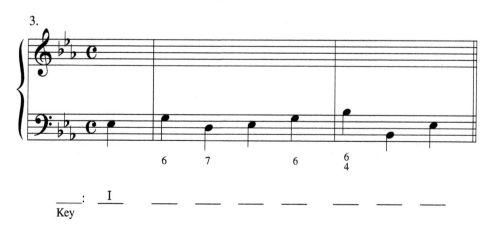

_____: I ___ ___ ___ ___ ___ ___ ___ ___
Key

I. Each of the following melodies is a folk song.

1. Play or sing each melody several times. Determine the harmonic rhythm and place a bracket above the melody tones that will be supported by each harmony.

2. Rewrite the melody on a separate sheet of score paper and indicate all possible triads that can harmonize the tones within each bracketed area.

3. Play or sing the melody again several times, experimenting with various harmonies. Indicate especially the points where a vii^{ø7} or vii^{o7} might occur.

4. Select the series of triads, dominant 7th chords, and leading-tone 7th chords you like best, and write them on the score paper beneath the melody.

5. Be sure that descending P5th (ascending P4th) progressions play a prominent role in each harmonization. Do not hesitate to exchange the vii^{ø7} or vii^{o7} for the V^7 where possible.

6. Select an accompaniment figure that can be used more or less intact throughout. The accompaniment figure should fit the medium (piano, stringed instruments, woodwind instruments, brass instruments, and so forth).

Block chord   Possible accompaniment chords for piano:

7. Fit the accompaniment figure to each successive chord and complete the composition.

8. Assign the melody itself to a solo instrument. If you wish, write words of your own for the folk song melody.

9. Play some of the compositions in class. The students can decide which harmonic rhythm and harmonization is most suitable to the particular melody.

1. Russian Folk Song.

2. American Folk Song.

3. American Folk Song.

4. American Folk Song.

J. Refer to page 219 for an excerpt from the third movement of Mozart's Piano Sonata in A Minor, K. 310.
  1. Listen to a recording or a classroom performance of the excerpt.
  2. Analyze each chord using macro analysis symbols:

> Major = Capital letter
> Minor = Lowercase letter
> Diminished = Lowercase letter plus °
> Augmented = Capital letter plus $^+$
> Major-minor 7th = Capital letter plus ^{7}
> Diminished-minor 7th = Lowercase letter plus ^{ø7}
> Diminished-diminished 7th = Lowercase letter plus $^{°7}$

  3. Add a solid slur between all circle progressions (for example, D^7 to g).
  4. Add a dotted slur between all leading-tone progressions (for example, $f\sharp^{°7}$ to g).
  5. For review and practice, indicate the phrases and the cadences.

K. Refer to the introduction to the *Pathétique* Sonata for Piano, op. 13, by Beethoven on page 179.
  1. Listen to a recording or have a member of the class play the excerpt.
  2. Do a complete macro analysis of the excerpt. Remember to add slurs to the circle progressions and leading-tone progressions.
  3. Place an X above each major-minor, diminished-minor, and fully diminished 7th chord.

L. Compose a short composition in the style of a folk song. A good example of the form described here is the "Wabash Cannon Ball." This melody can be found in Chapter 13, exercise H, on page 134.

1. Write two phrases using the following elements:

Phrase	Number of Measures	Relationship	Cadence	Type
1	4	a	half	
2	4	ap	authentic	parallel

2. Use either a major or minor key. Include at least one vii$^{\varnothing 7}$ or vii$^{\circ 7}$ (leading-tone 7th chord). If you lack ideas, start with the following chords:

Measures:	1	2	3	4	5	6	7	8
Chords:	e	d♯$^{\circ 7}$	e	B^7	e	a	B^7	e

3. Compose the melody to fit the harmony.
4. Convert the block chords to an accompaniment pattern for either guitar or piano.
5. Compose words for the melody (if you wish).
6. Perform each student composition in class. Have one student sing the melody while another plays the accompaniment.

Review

1. Practice spelling leading-tone 7th chords in all major and minor keys. Remember that the leading-tone seventh in major is half-diminished while that in minor is fully diminished. How is the half-diminished 7th chord indicated in Roman numerals? The fully diminished 7th chord?

2. Play the examples in Figure 12.15 (page 262 of the text) at the piano, observing the resolution of the 7th and the treatment of the tritones. Review the text associated with these examples.

3. Write the leading-tone 7th chord in a major or a minor key in four parts. Now resolve the chord to the tonic chord. The half-diminished 7th chord contains one perfect 5th (between the 3rd and 7th of the chord). Did you avoid parallel perfect 5ths in resolving this chord?

4. Look again at Figure 12.15 on page 262 of the text. Play examples a and b at the piano. Now transpose these two examples to the keys of E-flat major and E-flat minor. Next move them to E major and E minor. Continue transposing these examples until you have played them in all keys.

5. Review the figured-bass symbols for the inversions of 7th chords found on pages 236–237 of the text (Chapter 11). Now complete several of the figured basses that were not assigned, paying particular attention to the resolution of the 7th and the tritones of the leading-tone 7th chords.

Test Yourself 12

Answers are on page 241.

Number 1 below refers to this musical example:

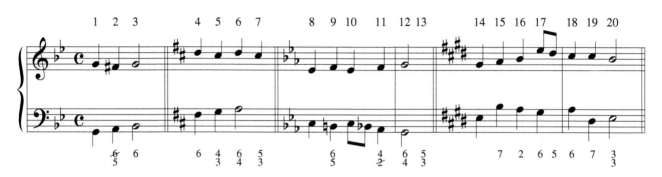

1. Place the twenty chords above in the following categories:

    a. Triad in root position _____

    b. Triad in first inversion _____

    c. Triad in second inversion _____

    d. V^7 chord _____

    e. vii°^{7} chord _____

    f. vii^{ø7} chord _____

Number 2 below refers to this musical example:

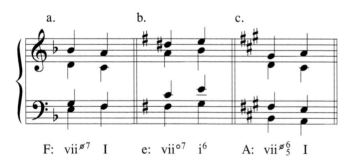

F: vii^{ø7} I   e: vii°^{7} i^6 A: vii$^{ø6}_{5}$ I

2. Each of the examples above contains an error in the resolution of the leading-tone 7th chord. Describe the error in each case.

    a. _____

    b. _____

    c. _____

CHAPTER 13
Nondominant Seventh Chords

A. Write the requested 7th chord in simple position above the given tone.

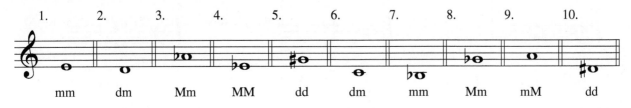

B. Provide the most common and often-used resolution for each of the 7th chords shown here. Analyze both chords in each exercise.

C. Give the chord analysis and the key (major and/or harmonic minor) in which the chord is diatonic.

1. (Ex.)

<u>vii°7</u> in the key of <u>E minor</u>

2.

_____ in the key of _____

_____ in the key of _____

3.

_____ in the key of _____

_____ in the key of _____

_____ in the key of _____

4.

_____ in the key of _____

_____ in the key of _____

_____ in the key of _____

_____ in the key of _____

5.

_____ in the key of _____

6.

_____ in the key of _____

_____ in the key of _____

D. Refer to the chorale "Werde munter, mein Gemüte," harmonized by Johann Sebastian Bach (1685–1750), on page 175.
   1. Analyze each chord using Roman numerals. Include also the proper designation for chord position (root position, first inversion, and second inversion).
   2. Circle and label each nonharmonic tone. Add the initials representing each nonharmonic device above or below the particular tone.

E. Each exercise is a phrase of a chorale melody with figured bass added. All were harmonized at least once by Bach.
   1. Add alto and tenor as required by the figured bass. Remember that figured-bass numbers indicate intervals above the bass note.
   2. Eighth notes in circles (as in nos. 1 and 4) are not to be harmonized.
   3. Chord no. 5 in chorale 4 contains a 7th that is delayed in resolution. The resolution occurs in the second chord following the 7th chord.
   4. Chords requiring other than first-choice doubling are indicated by special figured bass.
   5. Analyze each chord—blanks are provided.
   6. Arrange the chorale phrases for a quartet of instruments played by class members. Perform some of the harmonizations in class.

1. "Sei gegrüsset, Jesu gütig" ("Hail to Thee, Jesus Kind").

Bb: ___vi___ ___ ___ ___ ___ ___ ___ ___ ___ ___ ___

2. "Wach' auf, mein Herz" ("Awake, My Heart").

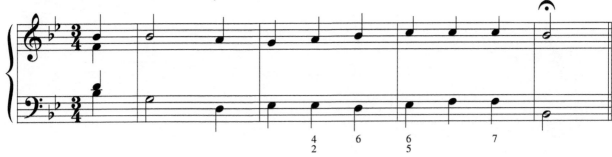

Bb: ___I___ ___ ___ ___ ___ ___ ___

3. "Du, o schönes Weltgebäude" ("Thou, O Fair Universe").

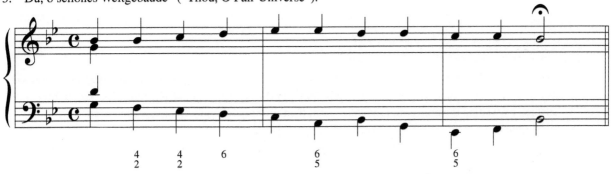

Bb: ___vi___ ___ ___ ___ ___ ___ ___ ___ ___

4. "O wie selig seid ihr doch" ("O How Blessed Ye Are").

F: ___vi___ ___ ___ ___ ___ ___ ___ ___

5. "O Mensch, bewein' dein' Sünde gross" ("O Man, Bewail Thy Great Sins").

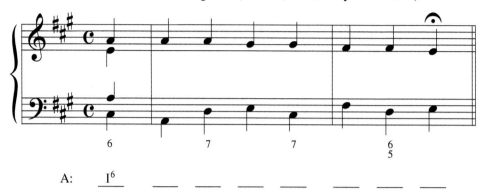

A: I⁶   ___   ___   ___   ___   ___   ___

6. "Jesu, meine Freude" ("Jesus, My Joy").

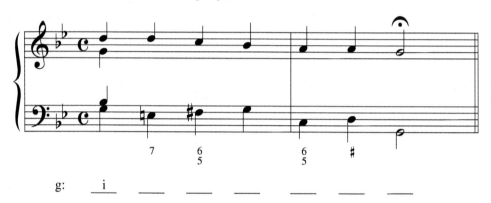

g: i   ___   ___   ___   ___   ___   ___

F. Each exercise represents a figured-bass voice.
   1. Complete the remaining three upper voices (soprano, alto, and tenor) according to the figuration supplied.
   2. Try to make each voice as interesting as possible, but the soprano should have priority. You will have the most success by writing the entire soprano voice first, then filling in the alto and tenor as needed.
   3. Be sure to observe voice-leading practices as cited in the text.
   4. Provide a complete Roman numeral analysis of each completed figured bass. Blanks are provided.

1.

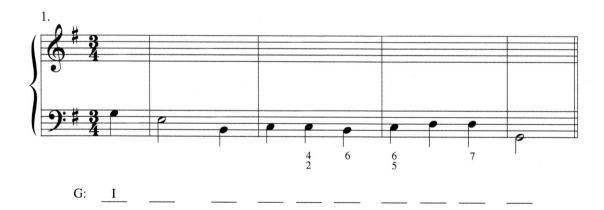

G: I   ___   ___   ___   ___   ___   ___

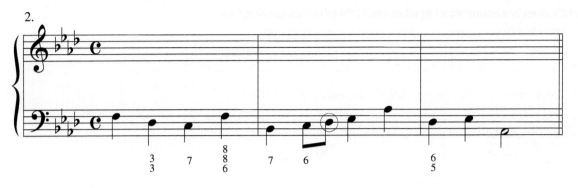

Ab: vi   _____   _____   _____   _____   _____   _____

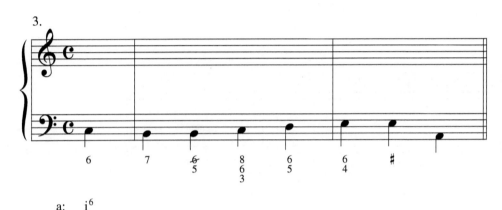

a: i⁶   _____   _____   _____   _____   _____   _____   _____

e: i   _____   _____   _____   _____   _____

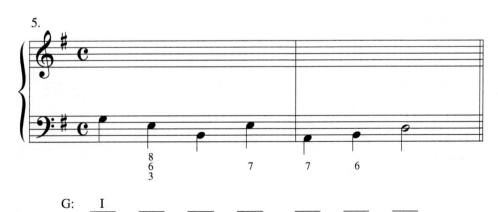

G: I   _____   _____   _____   _____   _____

G. Make a complete harmonic analysis of each of the following excerpts.
1. Provide a Roman numeral analysis that indicates inversions.
2. On the score itself, circle those tones you consider to be nonharmonic.

1. Bach: "Jesu, meine Freude" (motet), BWV 227, mm. 1–2.

2. Pachelbel: Chaconne in F Minor, mm. 1–9.

3. Kuhlau: Sonatina in C Major, op. 88, no. 3, III: Allegro burlesco, mm. 47–54.

4. Mozart: Sonata in F Major, K. 533, III: Rondo Allegretto, mm. 95–98.

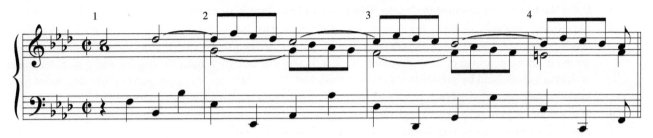

5. Bach (after Vivaldi): Organ Concerto in D Minor, BWV 596, IV, mm. 7–14.

H. Each of the following melodies is a folk song.

1. Using the procedures outlined in Chapter 10 on harmonic progressions, harmonize each of the folk songs below.

2. Experiment with fast, medium, and slow harmonic rhythms. Then select the one you prefer for each melody.

3. Write the accompaniment for guitar if the class has a guitar player. Have this student discuss writing accompaniments for the instrument. Range of the instrument, musical figures that lie easily under the fingers, and typical technical problems experienced by guitarists should be mentioned. If the class has no guitar-playing member, write for a piano or instrumental combo.

4. Write words of your own to each melody.

5. From the block chords of your harmonization, fashion an accompaniment that fits the medium you choose.

6. Perform the compositions in class. Have a voice student sing the melodies.

1. Russian Folk Song.

Try to use one nondominant 7th chord in the harmonization of the following melody.

2. Folk Song: "The Wabash Cannonball."

In the following folk song, try a harmonization made up *entirely* of 7th chords.

3. Folk Song: "Shady Grove."

Review

1. Study the chart of diatonic 7th chords in Figure 13.2 (page 272 of the text). While this chart appears quite complicated, observe that there is considerable duplication among the various scales. For example, the supertonic 7th chord is a minor 7th chord in major and the ascending minor scales. It is a half-diminished 7th chord in the natural and harmonic forms of the minor. Learn the Roman numeral symbols for each of the nondominant 7th chords.

2. Most nondominant 7th chords progress in a circle pattern. What chord will usually follow the supertonic 7th chord? The mediant 7th chord? The subdominant 7th chord? The submediant 7th chord? The tonic 7th chord?

3. Play the examples of nondominant 7th chord progressions in Figures 13.10 and 13.11 (page 277 of the text), observing the common pattern in the circle progressions involving the nondominant 7th chords in root position (Figure 13.10).

4. Write a mediant 7th chord in a major key in four parts. Resolve it in a circle progression to the submediant 7th chord. Continue the progression by resolving each 7th chord to another 7th chord in the circle pattern. Play the resulting progression at the piano. Repeat this pattern in minor, choosing the chords from the various forms of the scale that sound best to your ear.

5. Study the section on noncircle treatment of nondominant 7th chords on page 277 of the text. Do you observe any common pattern among these noncircle resolutions? Play the examples that illustrate each of these progressions (Figure 13.12).

Test Yourself 13

Answers are on page 241.

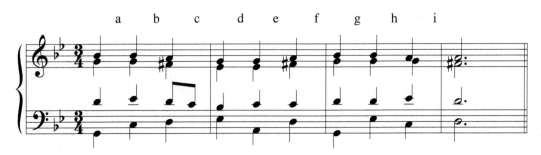

1. The chorale setting above contains a number of part-writing errors. Check each progression and describe any errors. There may be no errors, one error, or more than one error in any progression.

a. _____

b. _____

c. _____

d. _____

e. _____

f. _____

g. _____

h. _____

i. _____

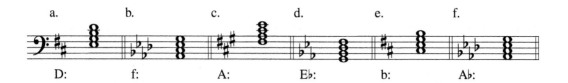

a.   b.   c.   d.   e.   f.

D: f: A: E♭:   b: A♭:

2. Each chord above is a nondominant 7th chord in the given key. Give the proper Roman numeral for the chord. If the chord is resolved in a circle progression, what chord would follow?

    a.   Roman numeral: _____   Roman numeral of following chord: _____

    b.   Roman numeral: _____   Roman numeral of following chord: _____

    c.   Roman numeral: _____   Roman numeral of following chord: _____

    d.   Roman numeral: _____   Roman numeral of following chord: _____

    e.   Roman numeral: _____   Roman numeral of following chord: _____

    f.   Roman numeral: _____   Roman numeral of following chord: _____

CHAPTER 14
Secondary Dominant and Leading-Tone Chords

A. Write the five secondary dominant chord types for the chord that appears at the end of each staff. Note the example.

B. Complete each exercise in the following manner:
1. Write the normal resolution for each secondary dominant or leading-tone 7th chord on the staff in four-part harmony.
2. Analyze the resolution chord in the blank provided.
3. Write the name of the key in the blank provided.
   The example demonstrates the correct procedure.

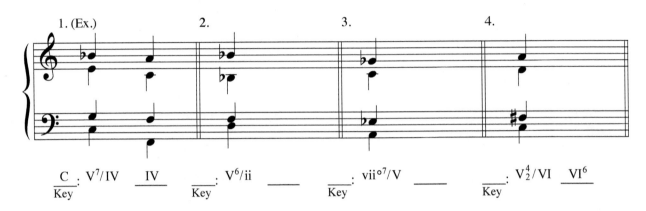

<u>C</u> : V⁷/IV   <u>IV</u>   ___ : V⁶/ii   ___   ___ : vii°⁷/V   ___   ___ : V₂⁴/VI   <u>VI⁶</u>
Key   Key   Key   Key

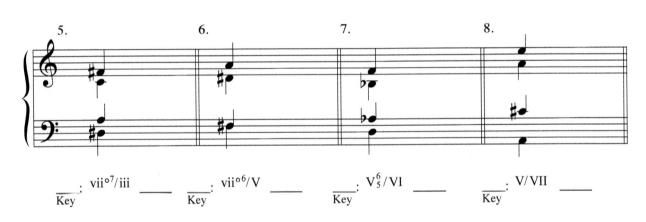

___ : vii°⁷/iii   ___   ___ : vii°⁶/V   ___   ___ : V₅⁶/VI   ___   ___ : V/VII   ___
Key   Key   Key   Key

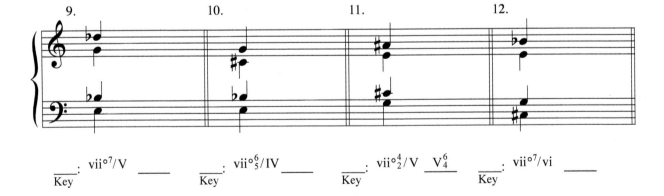

___ : vii°⁷/V   ___   ___ : vii°₅⁶/IV   ___   ___ : vii°₂⁴/V   <u>V₄⁶</u>   ___ : vii°⁷/vi   ___
Key   Key   Key   Key

C. Each secondary dominant or leading-tone chord below is analyzed in different keys, depending on the function of the chord to which it progresses. Assume in all cases that the resolution chord provides the most common type of progression for that particular chord. Name the key of the chord using the analysis given. Note the example.

1. (Ex.)

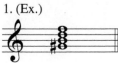

vii°⁷/V in the keys of ___D major and D minor___

vii°⁷/ii in the key of ___G major___

vii°⁷/iv in the key of ___E minor___

vii°⁷/VI in the key of ___C♯ minor___

vii°⁷/iii in the key of ___F major___

2.

V$^6_5$/V in the keys of _____

V$^6_5$/ii in the key of _____

V$^6_5$/iv in the key of _____

V$^6_5$/vi in the key of _____

V$^6_5$/iii in the key of _____

3.

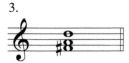

V⁶/ii in the key of _____

V⁶/VI in the key of _____

V⁶/iii in the key of _____

V⁶/V in the keys of _____

V⁶/IV in the key of _____

4.

vii°⁷/iv in the key of _____

vii°⁷/iii in the key of _____

vii°⁷/V in the keys of _____

vii°⁷/ii in the key of _____

vii°⁷/VI in the key of _____

5.

vii°⁶/iii in the key of _____

vii°⁶/V in the keys of _____

vii°⁶/ii in the key of _____

vii°⁶/iv in the key of _____

vii°⁶/vi in the key of _____

6.

vii°⁷/vi in the key of _____

vii°⁷/ii in the key of _____

vii°⁷/IV in the key of _____

vii°⁷/iii in the key of _____

vii°⁷/V in the keys of _____

D. Each exercise is a phrase of a chorale melody with figured bass added. All were harmonized at least once by Bach.
   1. Add alto and tenor as required by the figured bass.
   2. Analyze each chord. Blanks are provided.
   3. Arrange the chorale phrases for a quartet of instruments played by class members. Perform some of the harmonizations in class.

1. "Herzlich lieb hab' ich dich, o Herr" ("Dearly I Love Thee, O Lord").

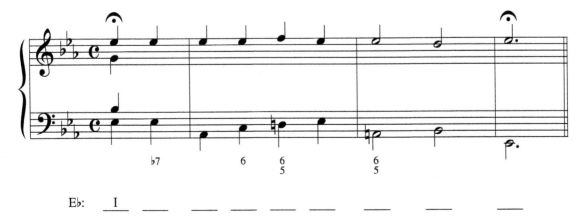

2. "Herr, wie du willst, so schick's mit mir" ("Lord, Ordain What Thou Wilt for Me").

3. "Valet will ich dir geben" ("I Wish to Bid You Farewell").

4. "Herr Christ, der ein'ge Gott'ssohn" ("Lord Christ, the Only Son of God").

d: V⁶/III   ___ ___ ___ ___ ___ ___ ___

5. "Warum betrübst du dich, mein Herz" ("Why Do You Grieve, My Heart").

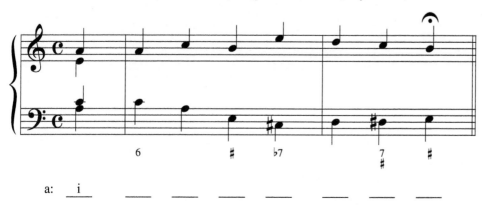

a: i   ___ ___ ___ ___ ___ ___ ___

6. "Wie bist du, Seele, in mir so gar betrübt" ("Why Art Thou, Soul, So Troubled Within Me").

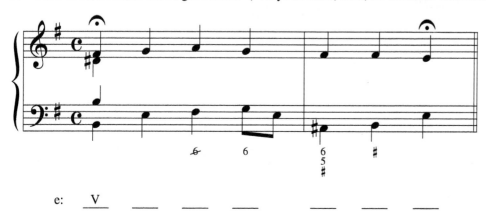

e: V   ___ ___ ___ ___ ___ ___

E. The following are additional chorale phrases. After completing the harmonizations, add at least four or five nonharmonic tones, including suspensions.

_____: ___ ___ ___ ___
Key

_____: ___ ___ ___ ___ ___
Key

_____: ___ ___ ___ ___
Key

_____: ___ ___ ___ ___ ___
Key

F. Each exercise represents a figured-bass voice.

1. Complete the remaining three upper voices (soprano, alto, and tenor) according to the figuration supplied.

2. Try to make each voice as interesting as possible, but the soprano should have priority. You will have the most success by writing the entire soprano voice first, then filling in the alto and tenor as needed.

3. Be sure to observe voice-leading practices as cited in the text.

4. Provide a complete Roman numeral analysis of each completed figured bass. Blanks are provided.

1.

2.

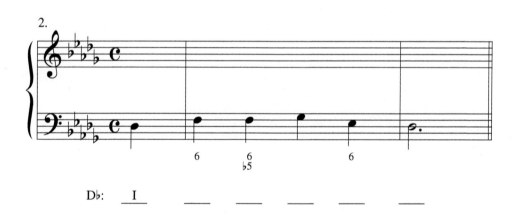

3.

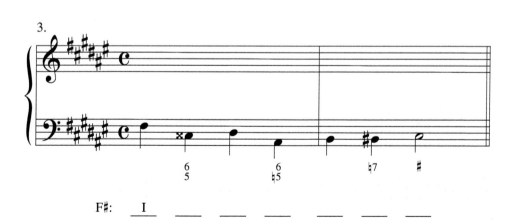

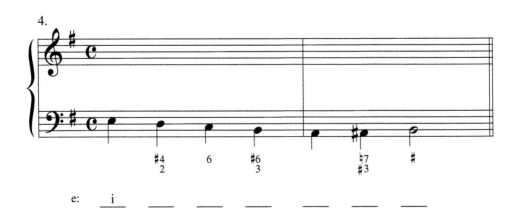

4.

e: ___i___ ___ ___ ___ ___ ___

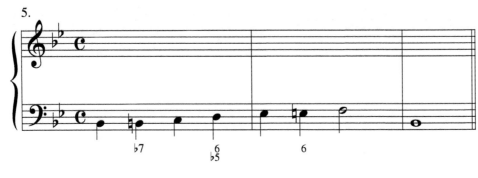

Bb: ___I___ ___ ___ ___ ___ ___ ___

5.

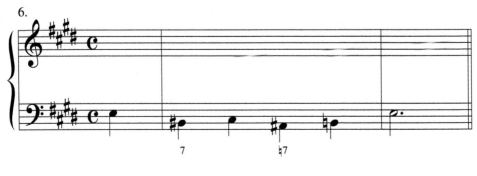

6.

E: ___I___ ___ ___ ___ ___

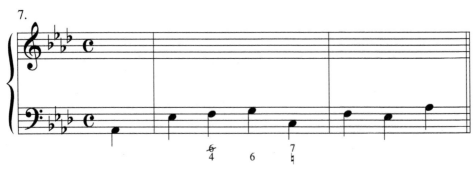

7.

Ab: ___I___ ___ ___ ___ ___ ___ ___

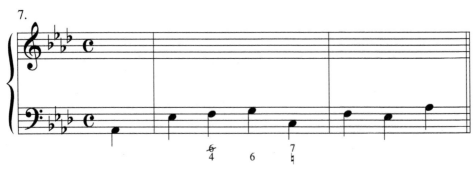

G. Do a complete harmonic analysis of each of the following excerpts from music literature.

1. Schumann: "Der arme Peter," op. 53, no. 3, from *Romanzen und Balladen*, mm. 1–4.

2. Debussy: *Claire de Lune* from *Suite Bergamasque*, mm. 1–12.

3. Brahms: Waltz in E Minor, op. 39, no. 4, mm. 1–10.

4. Schumann: Novelletten, op. 21, no. 8, *Fortsetzung und Schluss*, mm. 282–291.

H. On a separate sheet of paper, write a period consisting of two 4-measure phrases.

   1. Use the following chord progressions:

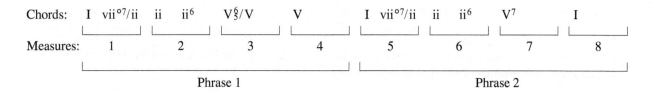

   2. Use the key of E-flat major and $\frac{6}{8}$ meter.
   3. Write in homophonic style (melody with chordal accompaniment).
   4. Make the two phrases parallel (measures 1 and 2 similar to 5 and 6, while 3 and 4 contrast with 7 and 8).
   5. Include at least one sequence.
   6. Compose your own theme (melody) or employ the following motive:

I. All accidentals have been deleted from this excerpt from Mozart's Symphony in G Minor. Add accidentals to create secondary dominant or leading-tone chords. Then check the score in your library to see what secondary dominants Mozart intended. Analyze your finished product.

Mozart: Symphony in G Minor, K. 550, IV: Allegro assai, mm. 1–8 (modified).

K. Refer to Schubert's Ländler, op. 171, no. 3, D. 790, on page 227.

1. Make a complete Roman numeral analysis and include indications for inversions.
2. Circle and identify all nonharmonic tones.
3. Analyze the phrase structure and identify cadences by type name.

L. The following excerpt is from the famous *Maple Leaf Rag*, written in 1899 by Scott Joplin (1868–1917).

1. Listen as a member of the class plays the excerpt.
2. Extract the melody only (the highest-sounding tones) and write it on the staves above each piano score.
3. On a separate sheet of paper, analyze the melody for the following:
   a. The phrases (length, number, and relationship of one to another);
   b. Characteristics of the melody such as syncopation, outlining of triads, nonharmonic tones, and so on.
4. Write a complete harmonic analysis (Roman numeral analysis).
5. In class, play or sing the extracted melody along with the extracted chords in simple position. Then have a member of the class play the excerpt as it was written by Joplin. Discuss the ways in which Joplin adapted the melody and block chords to pianistic writing.
6. Discuss the style (melodic, harmonic, and rhythmic) in relation to other popular styles with which class members are familiar.
7. Have a member or members of the class transcribe the excerpt for a small combo and perform it in class.

Joplin: *Maple Leaf Rag*, mm. 49–64.

V^9/V

M. Compose a short work of sixteen measures in the ragtime style for piano or for any combination of instruments played by class members. Use the excerpt from *Maple Leaf Rag* as a model for form and style.

N. Write a composition according to the following guidelines:
1. Sixteen measures in length.
2. In $\frac{6}{8}$ meter.
3. In harmonic rhythm primarily of one chord per measure (two chords per measure can be used in measures near the cadences).
4. In four phrases, with the following relationship:

Phrase	Type	Key	Cadence
1	*a*	G minor	Half cadence
2	*b* (contrast)	G minor	Authentic cadence
3	*a'*	G minor	Half cadence
4	*c*	G minor	Authentic cadence

5. For piano or an instrument with piano accompaniment.
6. Using at least three secondary dominant or leading-tone chords.

O. Refer to the third movement of Mozart's *Eine kleine Nachtmusik*, K. 525 on page 217.
   1. Make a complete harmonic analysis of the Menuetto (in G major) and the Trio (in D major).
   2. Discuss the use of:
      a. Secondary dominants
      b. Circle progressions
      c. Doubling and spacing in the chords

Review

1. Select a major key and write all the diatonic major and minor triads in that key (I, ii, iii, IV, V, vi). Now spell the secondary dominant and secondary leading-tone chords for each of these triads. Take note of the accidentals required for each of these chords. Only those chords that have accidentals outside the original key signature are considered secondary dominants or leading-tone chords.

2. Any major-minor 7th chord can be a secondary dominant in a number of keys. Select a major-minor 7th chord; spell the major and the minor triad it would normally resolve to (in a circle progression). List all the major and minor keys that contain the major or minor triad above. Analyze the given major-minor 7th chord in each of those keys.

   Example

Major-minor 7th chord:	G B D F (G⁷)
Resolves to:	C E G (C) or C E♭ G (c)
Keys containing C chord:	C major, G major, F major, A minor, F minor, D minor, E minor
Keys containing c chord:	B♭ major, A♭ major, E♭ major, C minor, G minor
Analyses of G⁷ chord:	

C: V^7	G: V^7/IV	F: V^7/V	a: V^7/III	f: V^7/V	e: V^7/VI
B♭: V^7/ii	A♭: V^7/iii	E♭: V^7/vi	c: V^7	g: V^7/iv	

3. Select a diminished 7th chord, spell the minor triad it would normally resolve to, then list the keys containing that minor triad. Analyze the given diminished 7th chord in each of those keys.

   Example

Diminished 7th chord:	B D F A♭ (b°⁷)
Resolves to:	C E♭ G (c)
Keys containing c chord:	B♭ major, A♭ major, E♭ major, C minor, G minor
Analyses of b°⁷ chord:	

B♭: $vii°^7/ii$	A♭: $vii°^7/iii$	E♭: $vii°^7/vi$	c: $vii°^7$	g: $vii°^7/iv$

Test Yourself 14

Answers are on page 242.

1. Each secondary dominant or leading-tone chord that follows is analyzed in different keys, depending on the function of the chord to which it progresses. Assume in all cases that the resolution chord provides the most common type of progression for that particular chord. Name the key of the chord using the analysis given.

Name_____

a.

vii°⁶/V in the keys of _____

vii°⁶/ii in the key of _____

vii°⁶/iv in the key of _____

vii°⁶/VI in the key of _____

vii°⁶/III in the key of _____

b.

V⁶₅/V in the keys of _____

V⁶₅/ii in the key of _____

V⁶₅/iv in the key of _____

V⁶₅/vi in the key of _____

V⁶₅/iii in the key of _____

c.

V⁶/ii in the key of _____

V⁶/VI in the key of _____

V⁶/iii in the key of _____

V⁶/V in the keys of _____

V⁶/IV in the key of _____

d.

vii°⁷/iv in the key of _____

vii°⁷/iii in the key of _____

vii°⁷/V in the keys of _____

vii°⁷/ii in the key of _____

vii°⁷/VI in the key of _____

2. Write the normal resolution for each of the 12 following secondary dominant and leading-tone 7th chords in four-part harmony. Be careful to properly resolve the active tones according to the voice-leading practices listed on pages 290 and 293 of the text. Name the key and provide a Roman numeral analysis of the resolution chord.

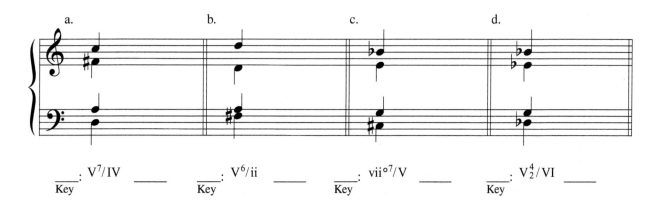

___: V⁷/IV ____   ___: V⁶/ii ____   ___: vii°⁷/V ____   ___: V⁴₂/VI ____
Key   Key   Key   Key

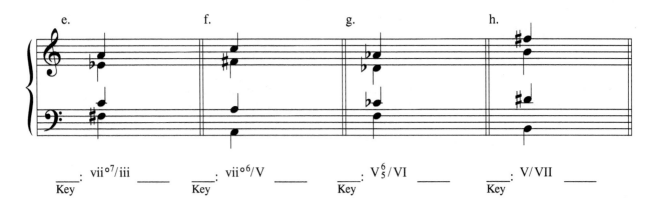

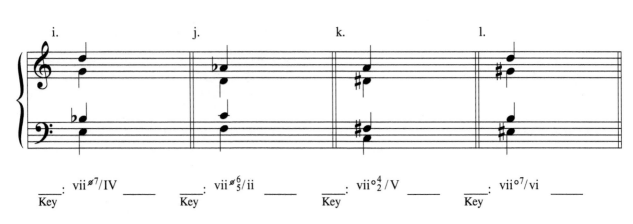

CHAPTER 15
Modulation

A. Each exercise is a chorale melody with figured bass. All have been harmonized at least once by Bach.

1. Add the alto and tenor voices according to the directions provided by the figured-bass symbols.
2. Make sure your part writing conforms to recommended practice.
3. Analyze each chord and indicate the point of modulation.

   a. If the modulation is of the common-chord type, bracket the pivot chord and analyze it in both keys.
   b. If it is a chromatic or phrase modulation, indicate the new key and continue analyzing in the new key.

4. Blanks are omitted to allow for proper bracketing in common-chord modulations.

1. "Ermuntre dich, mein schwacher Geist" ("Rouse Thyself, My Weak Spirit").

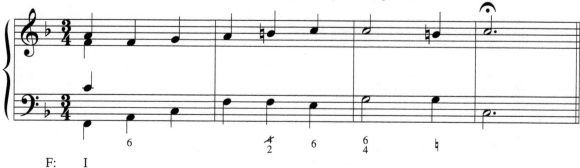

2. "O Jesulein süss, o Jesulein mild" ("O Sweet Child Jesus, O Gentle Child Jesus").

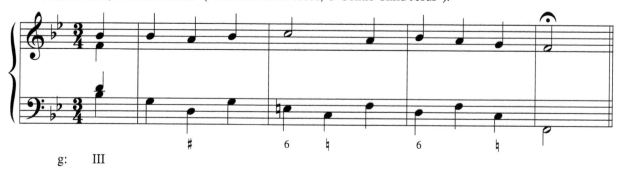

3. "Gott hat das Evangelium" ("God Gave the Gospel").

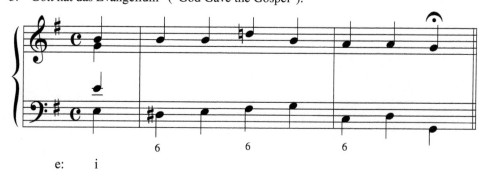

4. "Meines Lebens letzte Zeit" ("The Last Hour of My Life").

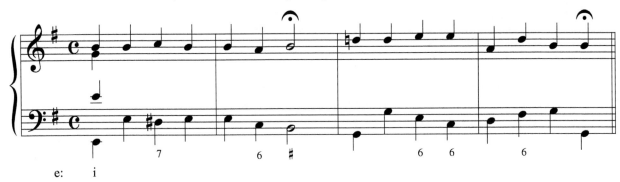

5. "Jesu, deine Liebeswunden" ("Jesus, Thy Dear Wounds").

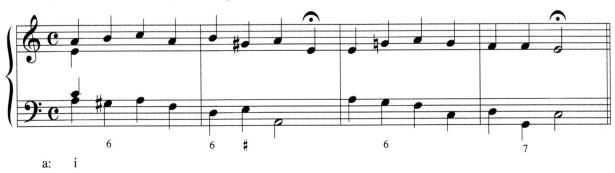

B. The following are additional exercises related to the exercises in A.

1. Add the alto and tenor voices according to the directions provided by the figured-bass symbols.

2. Make sure your part writing conforms to recommended practice.

3. Analyze each chord and indicate the point of modulation.

4. When completed, add at least four or five nonharmonic tones to each exercise.

5. Play these harmonizations in class and ask class members to determine which combinations sound most appropriate.

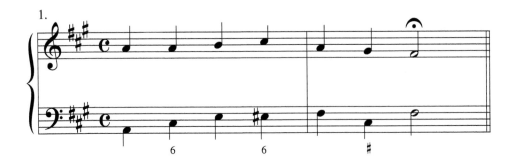

2.

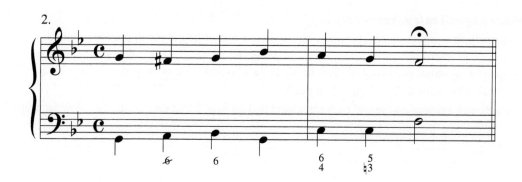

3.

4.

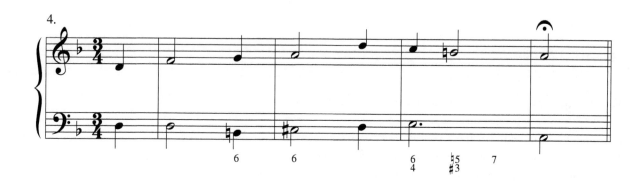

5.

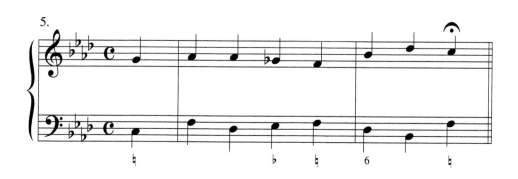

C. Each exercise represents a figured-bass voice.

1. Complete the remaining three upper voices (soprano, alto, and tenor) according to the figuration supplied.

2. Try to make each voice as interesting as possible, but the soprano should have priority. You will have maximum success by writing the entire soprano voice first, then filling in the alto and tenor as needed.

3. Be sure to observe part-writing practices as cited in the text.

4. Provide a complete Roman numeral analysis of each completed figured bass. Blanks are omitted to allow for proper bracketing.

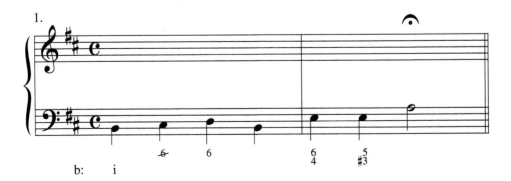

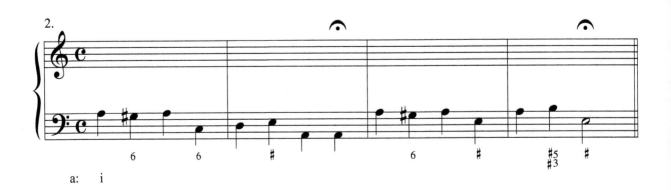

4.

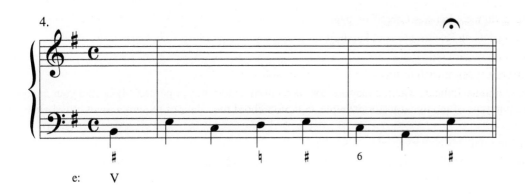

e: V

5.

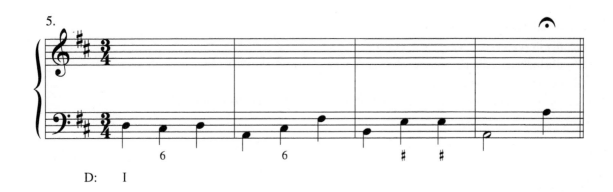

D: I

6.

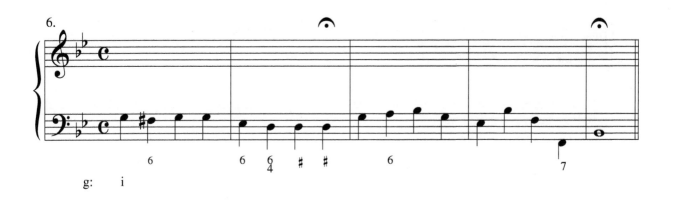

g: i

7.

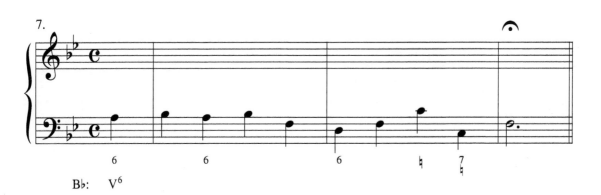

B♭:   V⁶

D. Refer to Bach's "Jesu, du mein liebstes Leben" on page 171.
    1. Analyze each chord using Roman numeral symbols.
    2. Circle and label all nonharmonic tones.
    3. Identify the cadence types at each fermata.
    4. Discuss the modulations. Indicate whether they are common chord, chromatic, or phrase. Make sure your analysis reflects the specific type of modulation (for example, common-chord modulations require a pivot-chord analysis that is bracketed).
    5. Enumerate the harmonic vocabulary used in this work.
    6. Divide the class into four sections (SATB) and sing the chorale. Have a conducting major conduct the performance.

E. Refer to Bach's "Straf' mich nicht in deinem Zorn" on page 174.
    1. Make a complete Roman numeral analysis of the chorale.
    2. Circle and label nonharmonic tones.
    3. Identify the cadence types at each fermata.
    4. Discuss the modulations. Indicate whether they are common chord, chromatic, or phrase.
    5. Divide the class into four sections (SATB) and sing the chorale.
    6. Arrange the composition for four instruments to be played by members of the class.

F. Following is the first phrase of the chorale melody, "O Haupt voll Blut und Wunden," composed by Hans Leo Hassler (1564–1612) and appearing for the first time in the year 1601. This melody became quite popular and was harmonized by a variety of composers, including Johann Sebastian Bach.

Hassler: "O Haupt voll Blut und Wunden" ("O Sacred Head Now Wounded"), mm. 1–2.

    1. Using the procedures outlined in Chapter 10 on harmonic progressions, harmonize this melody in four-part vocal style in the following four ways:
        a. First, harmonize the melody entirely in the key of C major.
        b. Next, harmonize the same melody entirely in the key of A minor.
        c. The third harmonization should begin in A minor and modulate to C major.
        d. The fourth harmonization should begin in C major and modulate to A minor.
    2. If you can, play each harmonization on the piano in four-part harmony. If you are unable to do so, play each in its block-chord form (chords in simple position).
    3. Determine which of the four you like best. Add appropriate nonharmonic tones to the four parts, distributing continuous eighth-note movement among the different voices.
    4. Each class member should put his or her completed harmonizations on the board or overhead projector. The entire class should then sing each one, conducted by a student.
    5. Return now to the block-chord version of the harmonization. Devise an appropriate instrumental accompaniment pattern that can be applied more or less to each chord. The following illustrations may provide ideas:

Simple accompaniment, two voices:

More complex accompaniment, two voices:

Melody with two-voice accompaniment (three voices):

6. Complete the chorale prelude (the chorale melody with the instrumental accompaniment pattern) for piano, organ, or instrumental ensemble and perform it in class.

G. Write a short composition of two phrases (eight measures).
    1. Write out the following chord progressions in block harmony (chords in simple position).

        Phrase 1   f: i   vii°⁷   i   i⁶   i⁶₄   V

        Phrase 2   f: i   vii°⁷   i   i⁶

                                    c: | V |
                                       | i | V⁷   i

    2. Each phrase should be four measures long in $\frac{6}{8}$ meter.
    3. The two phrases should be parallel (measures 5 and 6 the same or nearly the same as 1 and 2).
    4. Distribute the block chords in each phrase to produce musical balance.
    5. Above the chords, write a melody using essentially eighth-note movement.
    6. Write the composition for piano, solo instrument and piano, or for any combination of instruments played by class members.
    7. From the block chords, fashion an accompaniment to the melody. Make sure the accompaniment is appropriate for the medium chosen.
    8. Play the composition in class. If the composition is for a group of instruments, have a conducting student direct the performance.

H. Refer to Haydn's Sonata in E Minor, Hob. XVII:34 on page 212.
    1. Make a complete harmonic analysis of this excerpt.
    2. Analyze each modulation and decide if it is a common-chord, chromatic, or phrase modulation.
    3. Provide an analysis of the cadences, phrases, and periods.
    4. Listen as a member of the class plays the excerpt. Discuss your aural perception of the modulations. Do the key changes seem to occur abruptly or is there a gradual progression from one tonal center (key) to the next?

I. Write an original composition.
    1. Use a harmonic vocabulary that includes a variety of chord types studied to date.
    2. Use the following form:

Phrase Number	Relationship	Key	Cadence
1	*a*	D major	Half cadence in D major
2	*ap* (parallel to *a*)	Modulate from D major to A major	Authentic cadence in A major
3	*b* (contrasting)	Begin in F♯ minor and modulate to D major	Half cadence in D major
4	*a'* (parallel to *a*)	D major throughout (do not modulate)	Authentic cadence in D major

    3. Use homophonic texture (melody with chordal accompaniment).
    4. Write for piano alone or for a solo instrument with piano accompaniment.
    5. Although in writing for piano you may use a "broken" style (a style in which there is no set number of voices—you may range from three voices to five or six), use good part-writing procedures studied in four-voice chorale writing.
    6. Suggested steps in completing the composition:
        a. First, prepare a set of chord progressions for each phrase—chords that will accommodate the modulations easily. At this point, the chords may be simply blocked out with no voice leading present. Proper selection of the basic chords is most important and gives direction to the composition.
        b. Next, write a melody to fit with the chord progressions.
        c. Now change the block chords into a pianistic arrangement that flows well. One possibility is to use Alberti bass (the arpeggiation of blocked chords).
        d. Finally, add expression, tempo, and phrase markings to provide a musical interpretation.

Remember that composing is the technique of manipulating and arranging musical tones. Development of the skills required to prepare a composition is very important in understanding music.

J. Refer to the third movement of Mozart's String Quartet in G Major, K. 80, on page 222.
    1. Provide a harmonic analysis below each chord.
    2. Circle all nonharmonic tones.
    3. Identify the modulations as either common-chord, chromatic, or phrase modulations. Make sure your analysis style matches the modulation type.
    4. Discuss the harmonic vocabulary used in this work.
    5. Either listen to a recording of this quartet movement or have class members perform the work.

Review

1. Select a major or minor triad. List all major and minor keys in which that triad appears. (For example, the C-major triad appears in C major, F major, G major, A minor, F minor, and E minor). The triad can serve as a pivot chord in a common-chord modulation between any two keys. Select two keys on the list and analyze the selected triad in both keys.

2. Turn to the Bach chorale settings in the Anthology. Examine the beginning and end of each phrase to determine the key(s) at both points. If the key is different at the end of the phrase than at the beginning, complete a Roman numeral analysis to determine the point of modulation. Is the modulation a common-chord or chromatic modulation? (If you are not sure of the difference, see Figures 15.2 and 15.3 on pages 316–317 of the text, which illustrate each type.) Are there any examples of phrase modulation in the chorales? What is the difference between a phrase modulation and a common-chord modulation?

3. The diminished 7th chords are favorite vehicles for enharmonic modulation, since they may be spelled in a variety of ways. Select a diminished 7th chord and write at least four enharmonic spellings. For each spelling determine the key in which it would be the leading-tone 7th chord. This chord can function as a pivot chord between any two of those keys.

Test Yourself 15

Answers are on page 243.

1. Write all possible diatonic pivot chords between the given keys:

   a. Example: B♭ major and F major

B♭:	I	iii	V	VI
F:	IV	vi	I	ii

   b. D major and G major
   c. F♯ natural minor and A major
   d. E natural minor and C major
   e. F natural minor and D♭ major
   f. B major and D♯ natural minor
   g. G♯ harmonic minor and B major

2. Following are five chorale phrases that modulate. Provide a complete harmonic analysis for each phrase.

   a.

   Key____:

b.

Key____:

c.

Key____:

d.

Key____:

e.

Key____:

CHAPTER 16
Two-Part (Binary) Form

A. For each of the two-part compositions listed below:
1. Play the composition or listen to a performance.
2. Make a complete harmonic analysis of each composition.
3. Bracket each phrase.
4. Name the type of cadence at the end of each phrase.
5. Circle motives or themes that appear in both the A and B sections.
6. In your own words, indicate the relationship between the two sections.
7. Compare the form and construction of the compositions listed here.

Bach: Sarabande from French Suite no. 1 in D Major, BWV 812. (See page 176.)

Corelli: Corrente from Concerto grosso in F Major, op. 6, no. 9. (See page 188.)

Farnaby: "The New Sa-Hoo" from the *Fitzwilliam Virginal Book*. (See page 194.)

Handel: Gigue from Harpsichord Suite no. 7 in B-flat Major, G. 33. (See page 197.)

Handel: Sarabande from Harpsichord Suite no. 4 in E Minor, G. 166. (See page 205.)

Handel: Sarabande from Harpsichord Suite no. 5 in E Minor, G. 161. (See page 207.)

Haydn: Sonata in E-flat Major, Hob. XVI:28, II: Trio. (See page 211.)

Haydn: Sonata in E Minor, Hob. XVI:34, III: Vivace molto. (See page 212.)

Schubert: German Dance in D Major, D. 975. (See page 226.)

Schubert: Ländler, op. 171, no. 3, D. 790. (See page 227.)

Schumann: "Kleine Romanze" ("Little Romance") from *Album for the Young*, op. 68, no. 19. (See page 231.)

B. Write a composition using the following outline:

	Measures	Keys	Cadences	Phrase Relationships	Remarks
Part A	1–4	B♭ major	Half in B♭	a	
	5–8	B♭ major modulating to F major	Authentic in F	ap	Parallel structure
Part B	9–12	F major	Half in F	a'	Development of *a* motive or idea from phrase *a*
	13–16	F major modulating to B♭ major	Authentic in B♭	b	Different material

C. Write a composition in two-part form.
1. There are no restrictions on the content of this composition whatsoever, except that it must be in two-part form.
2. The composition should be of at least sixteen measures.
3. Write the composition for any instrument, voice, or combination of the two.
4. Play the composition in class.

D. Make a complete melodic, harmonic, and formal analysis of Brahms's "Sehnsucht" ("Longing") from *Songs and Romances*, op. 14, no. 8 on page 187.
   1. Have a member of the class play the accompaniment while a voice student sings the melody.
   2. Identify and label the modulations. The key relationships in this work are slightly complicated to assess. Explain why. What factors make identifying the tonal centers a challenge?
   3. Study the phrase relationships in this composition. After assessing the phrases, determine the form of the song.
   4. Write a short paper of 200–500 words summarizing the findings of your analysis.
      a. Describe how circle progressions, modulations, and key relationships shape the harmonic flow of the composition. Indicate if you discovered any secondary dominants or leading-tone 7th chords.
      b. Include information about phrases and the form.
      c. Indicate any other items you think are interesting.

Review

Chapter 16 deals with larger areas of musical structure and will require a new approach to study. Previous chapters required fluency in spelling chords and knowledge of the specifics of voice leading, which can be practiced, whereas this chapter requires an understanding of larger concepts and can be reviewed in much the same way you would review the materials of other textbooks.

1. Play or listen to a recording of each of the compositions analyzed in this chapter. Carefully examine the analysis of each composition, including the analytical statements in the scores themselves and the summary analysis that follows. Make certain that you understand each analytical statement. If certain items are not clear to you, reread the pertinent section of the chapter or look in previous chapters for an explanation. If you still have problems, discuss them with your instructor or a fellow student.
2. Define each term listed at the head of the chapter (page 339 in the text) in your own words. Compare your definition with the definition of the glossary and see if you can improve your definition. Consider how the terms can be applied to the compositions in the chapter.

Test Yourself 16

Answers are on page 244.

1. Examine measures 1–8 of Figure 16.4 on page 342 of the text. Would you describe the form of this section as open or closed? Why? What about the remaining section (measures 9–18)?
2. Examine measures 1–8 of Figure 16.5 on pages 343–344 of the text. Would you describe the form of this section as open or closed? Why? What about the remaining section (measures 9–34)?
3. We have used the terms *phrase, period,* and *section* to designate the elements of form. Define each of these terms to make a clear distinction among them. Can a phrase ever be a period? Can a period ever be a section? Why or why not?

CHAPTER 17
Three-Part (Ternary) Form

A. For each of the three-part compositions listed below:
1. Perform the composition on the piano or sing the entire work as written (sing the notes on a neutral syllable, such as *lu, la,* or *ta*).
2. Provide a complete harmonic, melodic, and formal analysis of each composition.
3. Compare the form and construction of the works listed here.
4. Have members of the class arrange the compositions for three or four instruments (such as a bassoon and two clarinets). Perform the arrangements in class.

Schumann: "Erinnerung" ("Remembrance") from *Album for the Young,* op. 68, no. 28. (See page 229.)

Beethoven: Sonata in E-flat, op. 31, no. 3, III. (See page 181.)

Grieg: "Volkweise" ("Folk Song"), op. 38. (See page 195.)

Schumann: "Fröhlicher Landmann" ("Happy Farmer") from *Album for the Young*, op. 68, no. 10. (See page 230.)

Schumann: "Wilder Reiter" ("Wild Rider") from *Album for the Young*, op. 68, no. 8. (See page 233.)

B. Write a short composition in three-part form.
1. Pattern the form after "Wilder Reiter" (section A above) by Schumann.
2. The composition should be homophonic (a clearly defined melody with harmonic and rhythmic accompaniment).
3. Use *only* the harmonic vocabulary studied to date.
4. Employ compositional procedures found in Chapter 10 of the textbook, "Harmonic Progression."
5. Write the composition for any instrument, voice, or combination thereof that class members can play.
6. When the composition is completed, each student should perform, or have his or her work performed, in class.
7. Each composition should be critiqued by class members.

C. The compositions listed below are examples of rounded binary (incipient three-part) form:
1. Provide a complete harmonic, melodic, and formal analysis for each composition.
2. Compare the construction of the compositions listed here.
3. Arrange one or more of the compositions for three or four instruments.
4. Perform the arrangements in class.

Beethoven: Thema from *Sechs Variationen* in D Major, op. 76. (See page 184.)

Corelli: Largo from Concerto grosso in D Major, op. 6, no. 1. (See page 190.)

Haydn: Sonata in C Major, Hob. XVI:35, III: Finale. (See page 213.)

Kuhlau: Sonatina in F Major, op. 55, no. 4, II: Andante con espressione. (See page 214.)

Mozart: Sonata in A Major, K. 331, I: Andante grazioso. (See page 221.)

D. Make a complete analysis of the Andante Cantabile, the second movement of the Sonatina, op. 88, no. 2, by Kuhlau (see page 215).
1. Analyze the harmonic, melodic, and formal elements of the movement.
2. Write a short paper of 200–500 words summarizing your analysis.
    a. Describe how circle progressions, chromatic chords, modulations, and key relationships shape the harmonic flow of the composition.
    b. Include information about motives, phrases, and the form.

Review

Chapter 17, like the previous chapter, deals with larger areas of musical structure. This chapter can be studied in much the same way as Chapter 16.

1. Play or listen to a recording of each of the compositions analyzed in this chapter. Carefully examine the analysis of each composition, including the analytical statements in the scores themselves and the summary analysis that follows. Make certain that you understand each analytical statement. If certain items are not clear to you, reread the pertinent section of the chapter or look in previous chapters for an explanation. If you still have problems, discuss them with your instructor or a fellow student.

2. Define each term listed at the head of the chapter (page 355 in the text) in your own words. Compare your definition with the definition of the glossary and see if you can improve your definition. Consider how the terms can be applied to the compositions in the chapter.

Test Yourself 17

Answers are on page 244.

1. Examine measures 1–16 of Figure 17.2 on pages 357–358 of the textbook. Would you describe the form of this section as open or closed? Why?

2. Examine measures 17–32 of Figure 17.2 on page 358 of the text. Would you describe the form of this section as open or closed? Why?

3. Describe the function of the B section of a three-part (ternary) form.

4. In this chapter a form called rounded binary form was discussed. How does the rounded binary form differ from a three-part (ternary) form?

5. A ternary form may be expanded in two ways: by repetition of a section or by the appearance of auxiliary formal members. Name three auxiliary members that may be added to the basic three-part design.

Anthology

Bach: "Christus, der ist mein Leben" ("Christ Is My Life"), BWV 281. ♪

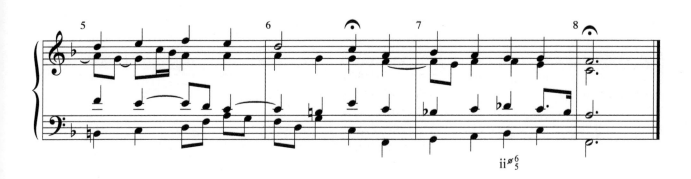

ii∅⁶₅

Bach: "Danket dem Herren, denn er ist sehr freundlich" ("Thank Ye the Lord, for He is very Gracious"), BWV 286. ♪

ii∅⁶₅

Bach: "Gottes Sohn ist kommen" ("The Son of God Has Come"), BWV 318.

Bach: "Jesu, du mein liebstes Leben" ("Jesus, Thou My Dearest Life"), BWV 356.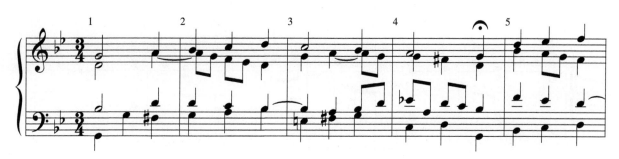

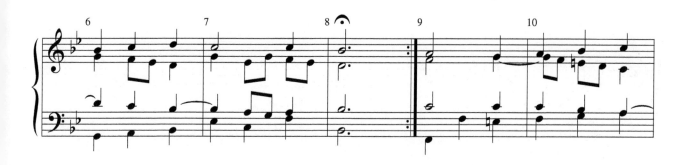

Bach: "O Ewigkeit, du Donnerwort" ("Oh Eternity, Thou Word of Thunder"), BWV 20.

Bach: "O Herre Gott, dien göttlich Wort" ("Oh Lord Our God, Thy Holy Word"), BWV 184.

Bach: "Straf' mich nicht in deinem Zorn" ("Punish Me Not in Thy Wrath"), BWV 115. ♪♪

Bach: "Werde munter, mein Gemüte" ("Sink Not Yet, My Soul to Slumber"), BWV 55. ♫

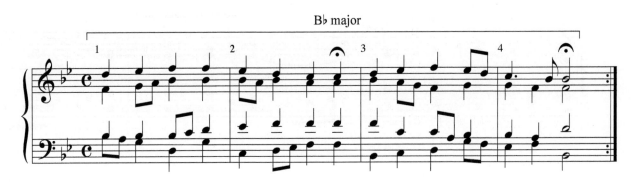

B♭: __ __ __ __ __

c: __ __ __ __ __ __ __   E♭: __ __ __ __ __ __

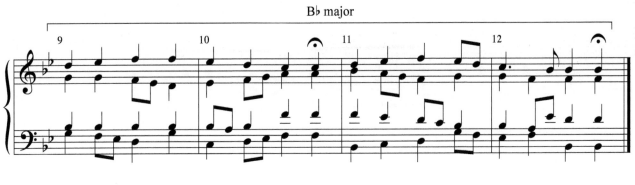

B♭: __ __ __ __ __

Bach: Sarabande from French Suite no. 1 in D Minor, BWV 812.

Bartók: Bagatelle, op. 6, no. 5, mm. 30–47. ♪♪

Bartók: "Rumanian Folk Song" from *Sketches*, op. 9b, no. 5.

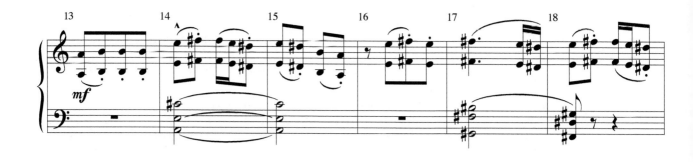

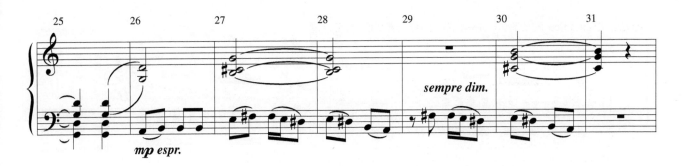

Beethoven: Sonata in C Minor *(Pathétique),* op. 13, I, mm. 1–11. ♫

attacca subito il Allegro

Beethoven: Sonata in E-flat Major, op. 31, no. 3, III. ♪

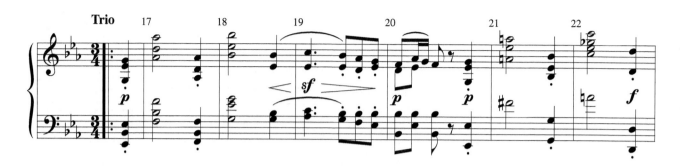

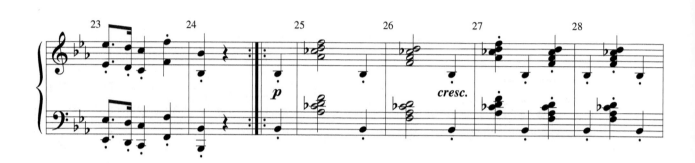

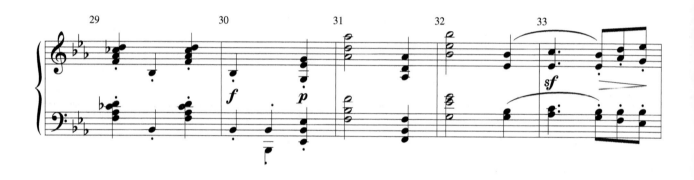

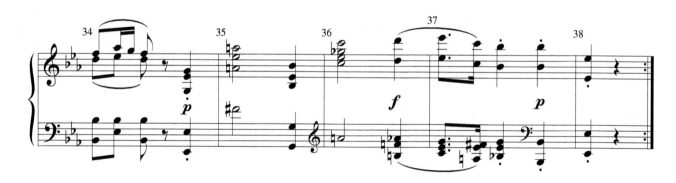

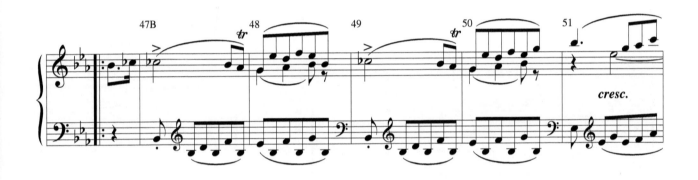

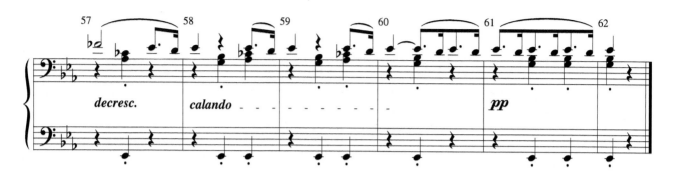

Beethoven: Thema from *Sechs Variationen* in D Major, op. 76. ♪

Brahms: "Ich schell mein Horn ins Jammertal," op. 43, no. 3.

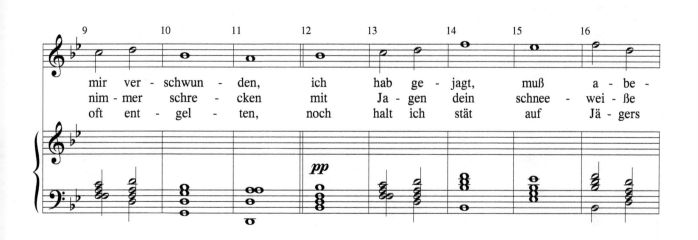

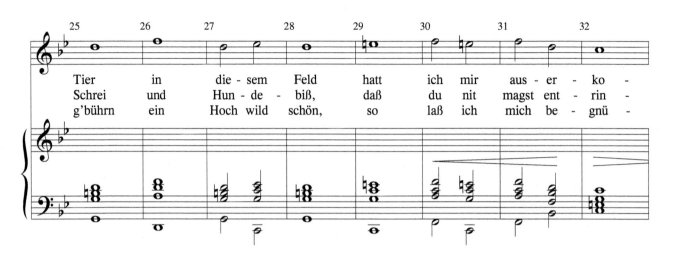

Brahms: "Sehnsucht" ("Longing") from *Songs and Romances*, op. 14, no. 8.

Mein Schatz ist nicht da, ist weit ü - berm See und so

oft ich dran denk, tut mir's Her - ze so weh! Schön blau ist der

See und mein Herz tut mir weh, und mein Herz wird nicht g'sund, bis mein

Schatz wie-der kommt! Schön blau ist der See und mein Herz tut mir

weh, und mein Herz wird nicht g'sund, bis mein Schatz wie-der kommt!

Corelli: Corrente from Concerto grosso in F Major, op. 6, no. 9.

Corelli: Largo from Concerto grosso in D Major, op. 6, no. 1.

Couperin: Rigaudon from *Pièces de clavecin* (Pieces for the Harpsichord), Second Order. ♪

Interval between highest and lowest voice:

P8	m3	m3	P5	P8												
1	2	3	4	5	6	7	8	9	10	11	12	13	14	15	16	17

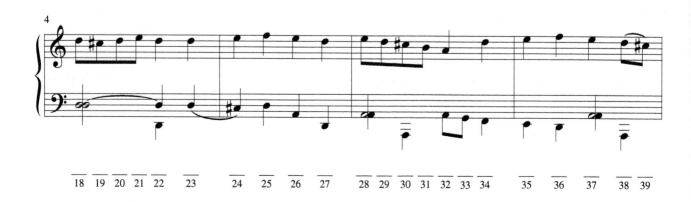

18 19 20 21 22   23   24 25 26 27   28 29 30 31 32 33 34   35   36   37   38 39

40   41   42   43   44   45   46   47   48 49 50 51 52   53   54   55   56   57 58

59   60 61 62 63   64   65   66   67   68   69   70   71   72   73   74   75   76 77

78 79 80 81 82 83   84 85 86 87   88 89 90 91 92 93 94 95 96 97 98 99 100 101

Crüger: "Herr, ich habe missgehandelt" ("Lord, I have Transgressed").

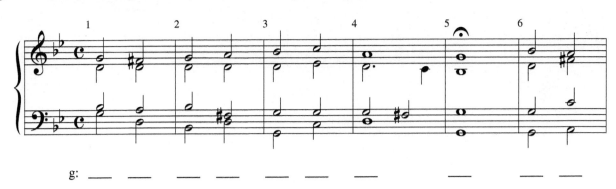

g: ___ ___ ___ ___ ___

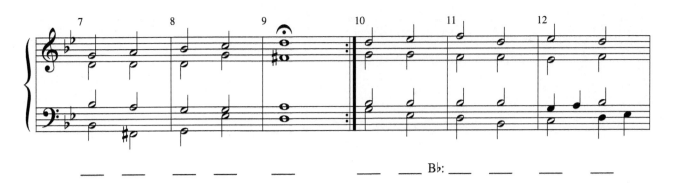

___ ___ ___ ___ ___ ___ ___ B♭: ___ ___ ___

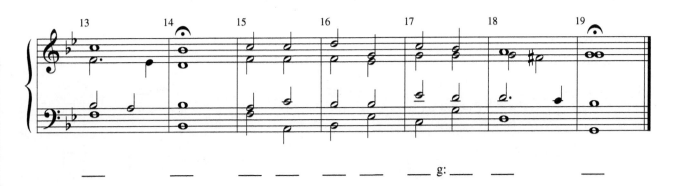

___ ___ ___ ___ ___ ___ g: ___ ___ ___

Farnaby: "The New Sa-Hoo" (written circa 1595) from the *Fitzwilliam Virginal Book.* ♪♪

Grieg: "Volkweise" ("Folk Song") from *Lyric Pieces*, op. 38, no. 2.

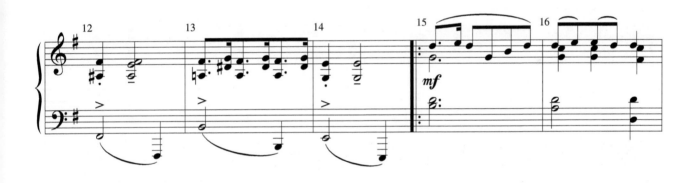

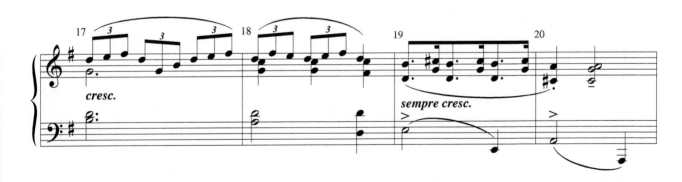

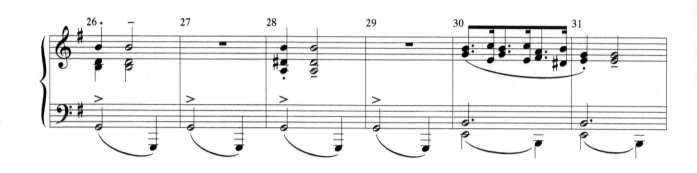

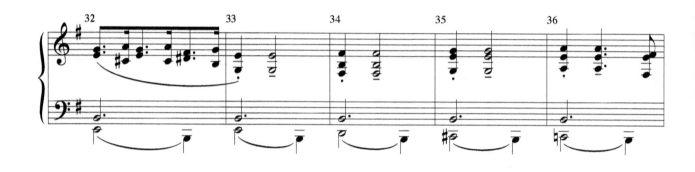

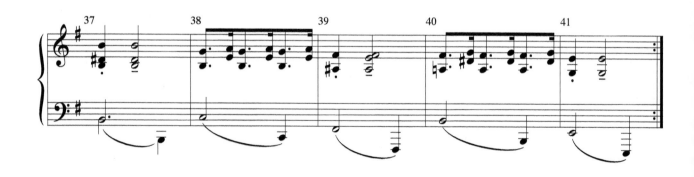

Handel: Gigue from Harpsichord Suite no. 7 in B-flat Major, G. 33.

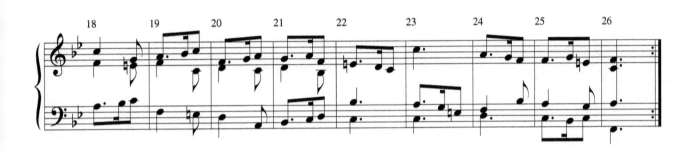

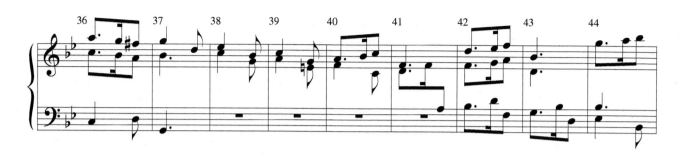

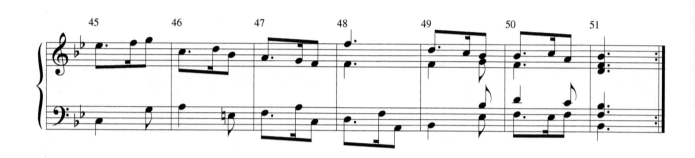

Handel: "Hallelujah!" from *Messiah* (choral parts only).

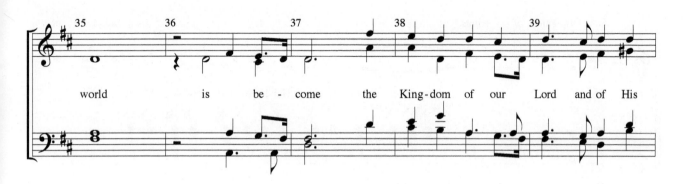

world   is   be - come   the   King - dom of our   Lord and of His

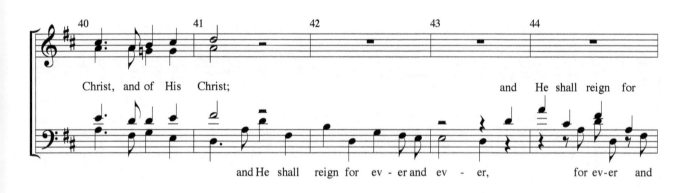

Christ, and of His   Christ;   and   He shall reign for

and He shall   reign for ev - er and ev -   er,   for ev-er and

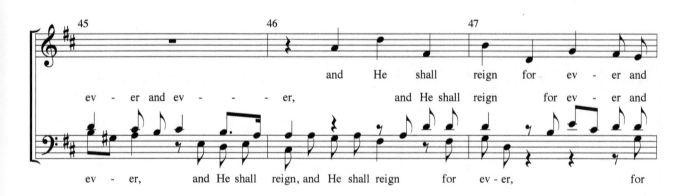

                and   He   shall   reign   for   ev - er and

ev - er and ev -   er,   and He shall reign   for ev - er and

ev - er,   and He shall reign, and He shall reign   for   ev - er,   for

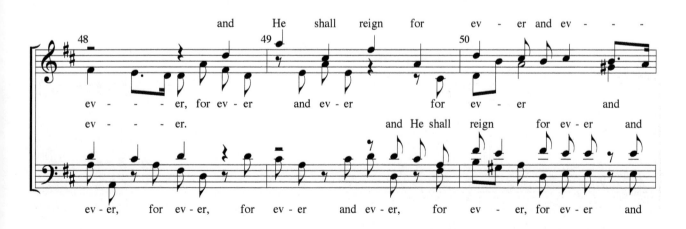

               and   He   shall   reign   for   ev - er and ev - - -

ev - - - er, for ev - er   and ev - er   for ev - er   and

ev - - - er.   and He shall   reign   for ev - er   and

ev - er,   for ev - er,   for ev - er   and ev - er,   for   ev - er, for ev - er   and

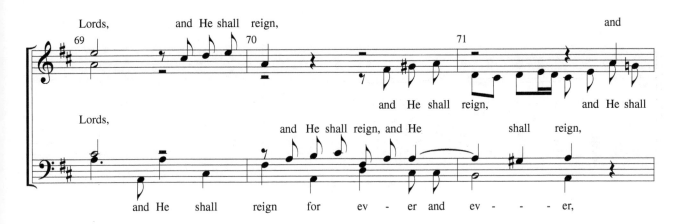

ev - er and ev - er, King of Kings, and Lord of Lords, King of

ev - er and ev - er,

Kings, and Lord of Lords, and He shall reign for ev - er and ev -

and He shall reign for ev - er, for ev - er and ev -

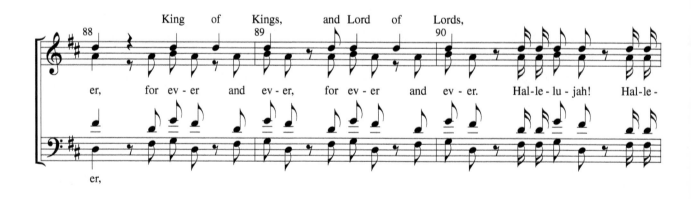

King of Kings, and Lord of Lords,

er, for ev - er and ev - er, for ev - er and ev - er. Hal-le - lu - jah! Hal-le -

er,

lu - jah! Hal-le - lu - jah! Hal-le - lu - jah! Hal - le - lu - jah!

Name_____

Handel: Sarabande from Harpsichord Suite no. 4 in E Minor, G. 166. ♫

Name_____

Handel: Sarabande from Harpsichord Suite no. 5 in E Minor, G. 161.

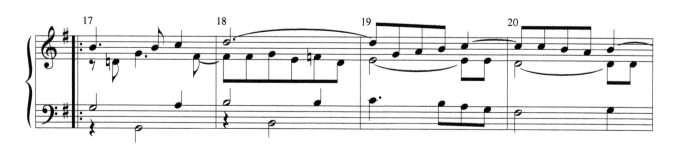

Haydn: Sonata in E Major, Hob. XVI:13, II: Menuet and Trio.

Trio

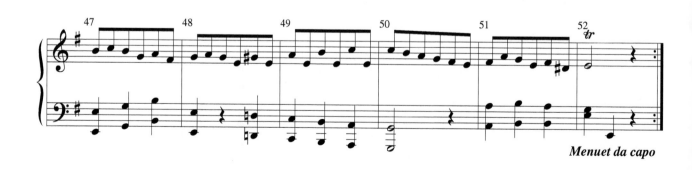

Menuet da capo

Haydn: Sonata in E-flat Major, Hob. XVI:28, II: Trio.

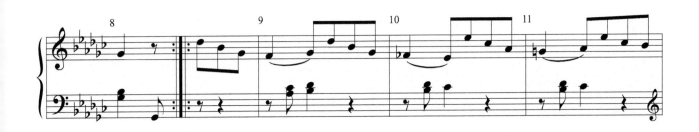

Haydn: Sonata in E Minor, Hob. XVI:34, III. ♫

Haydn: Sonata in C Major, Hob. XVI:35, III: Finale. ♪

Kuhlau: Sonatina in F Major, op. 55, no. 4, II.

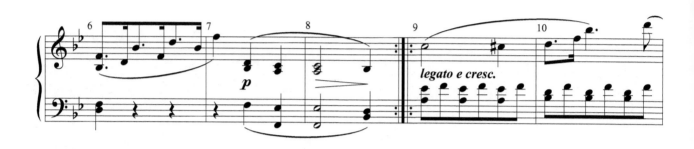

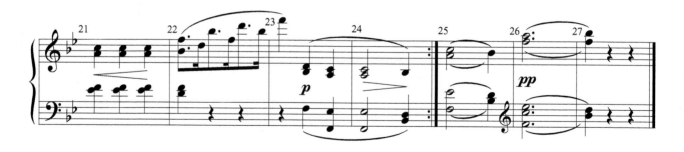

Kuhlau: Sonatina in G Major, op. 88, no. 2, II.

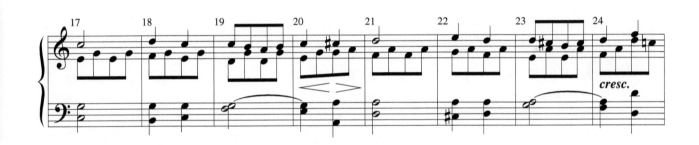

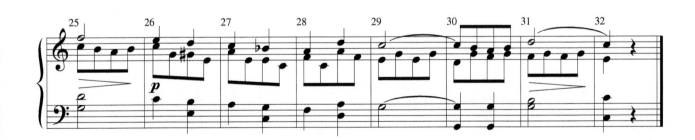

Lowell Mason: "Joy to the World!" (attributed to Handel). ♩♪

Joy to the world! the Lord is come: Let earth re-

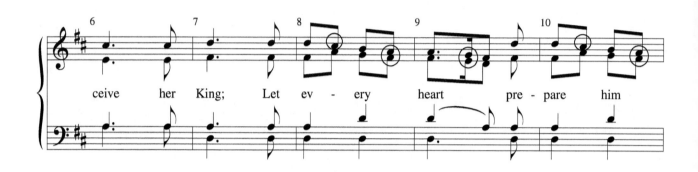

ceive her King; Let ev - ery heart pre - pare him

room, And heaven and na - ture sing, And heaven and na - ture

And heaven and na - ture sing, And

sing, And heaven, and heaven and na - ture sing.

heaven and na - ture sing,

216 Anthology

Mozart: *Eine kleine Nachtmusik,* K. 525, III.

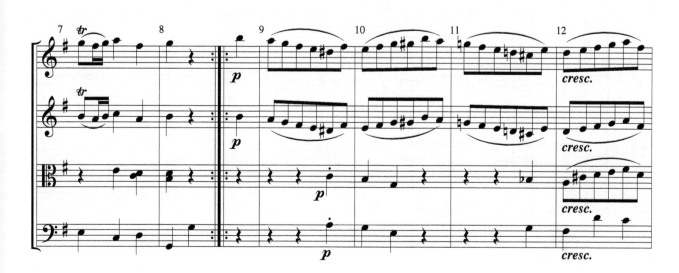

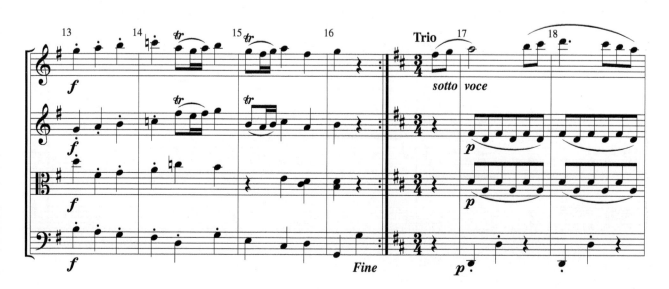

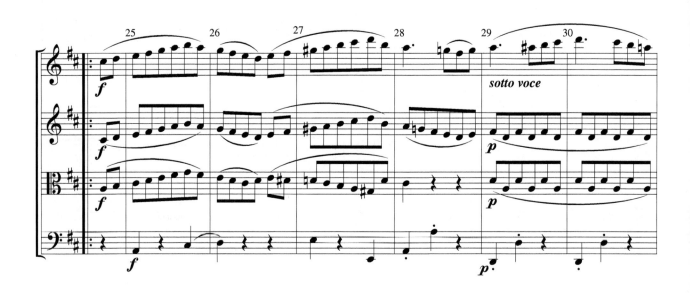

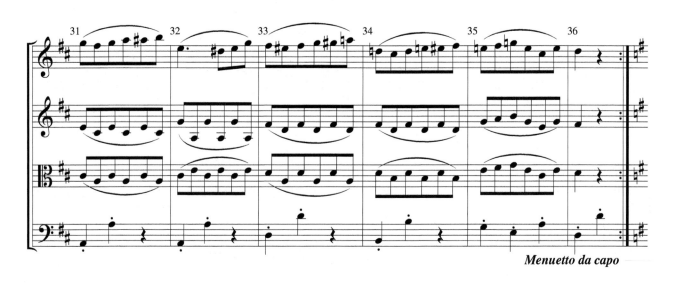

Menuetto da capo

Mozart: Sonata in A Minor, K. 310, III: Presto, mm. 183–252. ♪

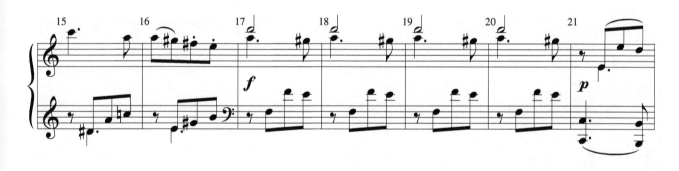

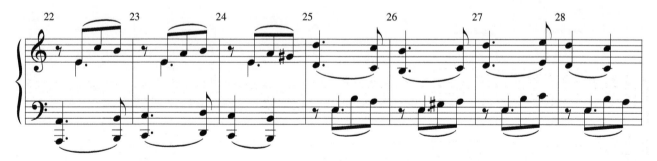

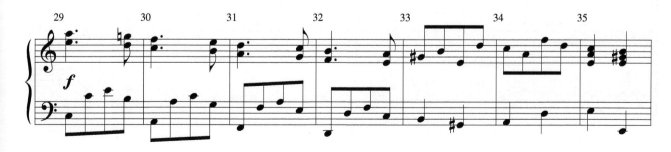

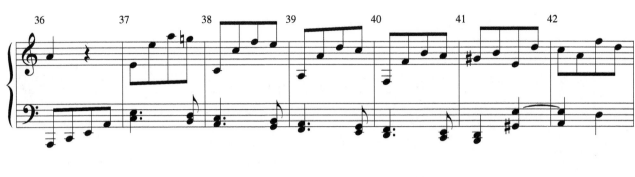

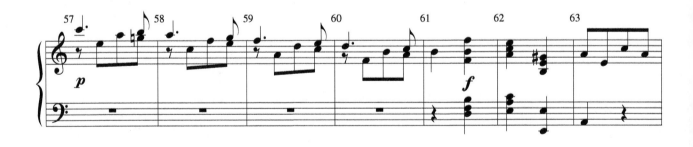

Mozart: Sonata in A Major, K. 331, I.

Mozart: String Quartet in G Major, K. 80, III: Menuetto.

Menuetto da capo

Nicolai: "Wachet auf, ruft uns die Stimme" ("Awake! Cries to Us the Voice"). ♪♪

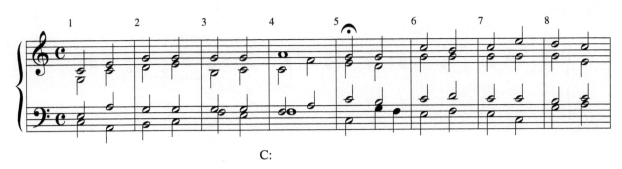

C:

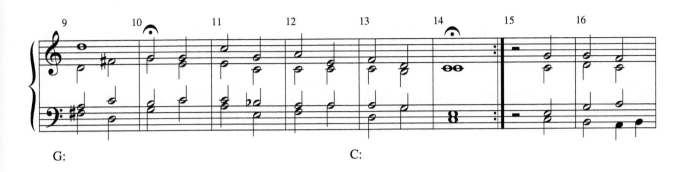

G: C:

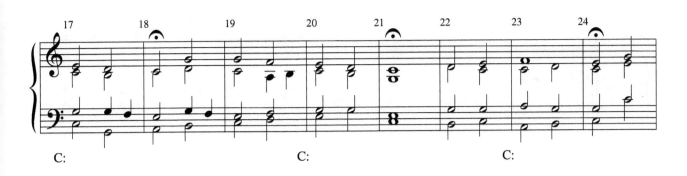

C: C: C:

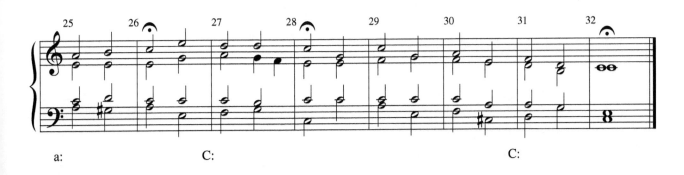

a: C: C:

Schubert: German Dance in D Major, D. 975. ♪♪

Schubert: Ländler in D Major, op. 171, no. 3, D. 790.

Schumann: "Ein Choral" ("A Chorale") from *Album for the Young*, op. 68, no. 4. ♫

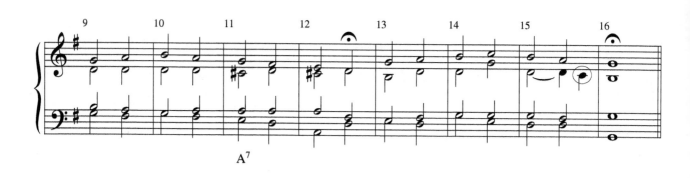

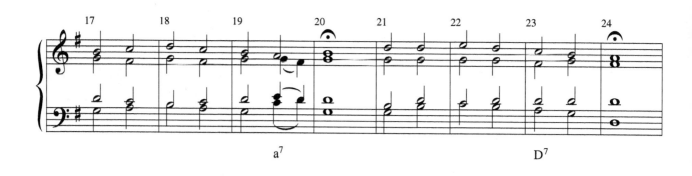

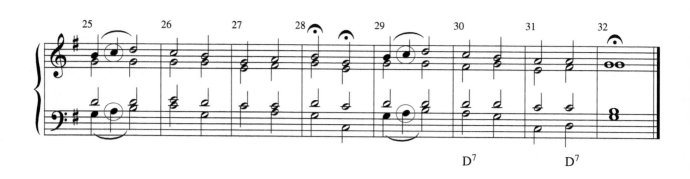

Schumann: "Erinnerung" ("Remembrance") from *Album for the Young*, op. 68, no. 28.

Schumann: "Fröhlicher Landmann" ("Happy Farmer") from *Album for the Young*, op. 68, no. 10. ♫

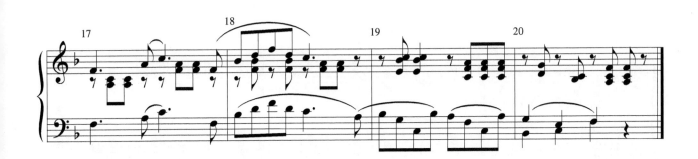

Schumann: "Kleine Romanze" ("Little Romance") from *Album for the Young*, op. 68, no. 19.

Schumann: "Wilder Reiter" ("Wild Rider") from *Album for the Young*, op. 68, no. 8.

Answers to Self-Tests

Test Yourself 1
page 6

1. The following answers correspond with the International Acoustical Society recommendations for octave identification (see Figure 1.9 on page 6 of the text):
    a. E4   b. D5   c. B2   d. E2   e. F4   f. F3   g. E3   h. G4   i. C6   j. G3   k. A1   l. F4

    An alternative version of these answers is as follows (see Figure 1.10 on page 7 of the text):
    a. e^1 b. d^2 c. B   d. E   e. f^1 f. f   g. e   h. g^1 i. c^3 j. g   k. AA   l. f^1

2. Pairs: (a–i) (b–d) (c–h) (e–g) (f–j)

3. a. Forte should not be on the staff.

    b. 1. Improper beaming. (Should be in groups of two eighth notes or all notes beamed together.)
        2. Stem direction should be down above the third line of the staff.

    c. Improper beaming. (First eighth note should not be beamed with the others.)

    d. Half rest should not be used in this location. (Should be two quarter rests.)

    e. 1. Notes in first chord not in proper relationship. (C should be to the left of the stem and D to the right.)
        2. Crescendo should be below the staff.
        3. Chord on the second beat of the measure should be notated as a quarter tied to an eighth to show the third beat of the measure.
        4. Stem direction should be up on the chord on beat four.

    f. Not enough beats in this measure.

    g. The dotted half rest should not be used here. (Should be quarter rest followed by half rest to show the third beat of the measure.)

4. Notes in parentheses are enharmonic equivalents.
    a. D (E♭♭)   b. G (F×)   c. C (B♯)   d. G (A♭♭)   e. F (E♯)   f. A (B♭♭)

Test Yourself 2
page 15

1. a. D harmonic minor   b. E major
    c. F natural minor   d. G melodic minor (ascending)

2. a. D major   b. E♭ major   c. D♭ major   d. E major
        B minor   C minor   c. B♭ minor   C♯ minor

3. a. C and F   b. D and A   c. B♭ and E♭   d. G and D

4. a. B   b. B♭   c. E♭   d. E

5. a. B♭ minor   b. D major   c. C♯ major   d. F♯ major

6. a. whole tone   b. pentatonic
    c. minor   d. pentatonic

7. a. Lydian   b. Dorian
    c. Mixolydian   d. Phrygian

Test Yourself 3
page 26

1. P1, m3, M3, P5, m6, M6, P8.

2. a. M3   b. M7   c. P4   d. m6   e. m2   f. A4

3. a. m6   b. m2   c. P5   d. M3   e. M7   f. d5

4. a. P1   b. M2   c. m3   d. M3   e. M6   f. m7
   g. m6   h. m10 (m3)   i. m6   j. m3   k. P4   l. m7
   m. m3   n. M2   o. m6   p. M3

5. a. D♯   b. C𝄪   c. A   d. F   e. B♭   f. D♯

6. a. C♯   b. A♭   c. B♭♭   d. C♯   e. D𝄪   f. A♭♭

Test Yourself 4
page 31

1. a. major   b. minor   c. augmented   d. diminished   e. minor   f. major

2. a. A   b. b   c. A♭+   d. d°   e. g   f. D♭

3. a. tonic I^6
   b. subdominant   IV
   c. leading tone $vii°^6$
   d. tonic   I
   e. dominant V^6
   f. tonic   I
   g. tonic I^6_4
   h. dominant   V
   i. tonic   I

4. a. V   b. VI   c. IV
   d. III   e. I   f. VII

5. a. vi   b. iv   c. ii
   d. v   e. iii   f. i

6. a. A$_{MI}$ b. E♭   c. B   d. C♯$_{MI}$ e. B♭+   f. E$^{dim.}$

Test Yourself 5
page 40

1. Deceptive
2. Perfect Authentic
3. Plagal
4. Deceptive
5. Half
6. Half
7. Half
8. Imperfect Authentic
9. Imperfect Authentic

10. Plagal
11. Perfect Authentic
12. Deceptive
13. Half
14. Plagal
15. Perfect Authentic

16. a. Plagal   b. Deceptive   c. Half   d. Perfect Authentic   e. Imperfect Authentic

17. a. Accented passing tone   b. 4–3 Suspension   c. Anticipation   d. 4–3 Suspension
     e. Unaccented passing tone   f. Appoggiatura   g. 7–6 Suspension

Test Yourself 6
page 58

Term	Can be found in (lines and numbers)
1. Internal extension of a phrase (example)	Line A, numbers 5–8; line A, numbers 9–12
2. Parallel period	A1–24 and B1–24
3. A sequence of two segments of one-half measure each	A13–16 and B13–16
4. A retardation	B21–23
5. An appoggiatura	A15, B15, C15
6. A 4–3 suspension	A21, B21 (inner voice)
7. A sequence of two segments of one full measure each	E1–8
8. An authentic cadence on F major	B19–23
9. A half cadence in C major	C21–23
10. Exact melodic repetition	A1–17 and B1–17
11. A 7–6 suspension	A5, A9, B5, B9, D11
12. A lower neighboring tone	C17
13. An accented passing tone	C11, C20, E10
14. A second-inversion triad	B19, C21, D3, E11
15. An imperfect authentic cadence in C major	E12–16
16. A phrase member	D1–8, D9–16, E1–8, E9–16
17. A phrase extension near the beginning	A5–8, B5–8
18. A set of contrasting phrases (period)	C1–23, C24–D16

19. four
20. two
21. The first one is a contrasting period, and the second one is a parallel period.

22. German Folk Song.

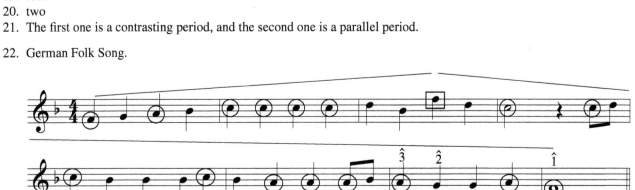

Test Yourself 7

page 62

1. monophonic texture: d
   polyphonic texture: c
   homophonic texture: b
   homorhythmic texture: a

2. primary melody (PM):   1, 3, 6, 7
   secondary melody (SM):   5
   parallel supporting melody (PSM): 2
   static support (SS):   no examples
   harmonic support (HS):   no examples
   rhythmic support (RS):   no examples
   harmonic rhythmic support (HRS): 4

3. The thinnest texture is example: d

4. The thickest texture is example: a

5. Beethoven: Sonata, op. 13, III: Allegro, mm. 1–8.

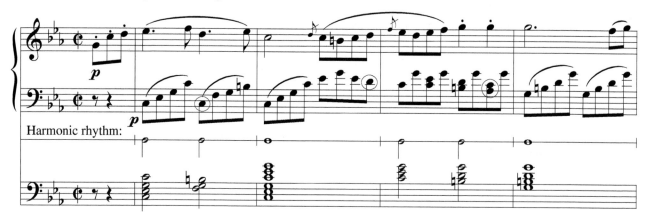

6. The right hand part in the preceding example is: PM (textural element).
   The left hand part is: HRS (textural element).
   The excerpt is an example of: homophonic texture (texture type).

Test Yourself 8

page 74

1. a. P1   b. m3   c. M3   d. P5   e. m6   f. M6   g. P8
   h. m10   i. M10

2. Unaccented passing tone.

3. a. unaccented passing tone   b. accented passing tone   c. upper neighboring tone
   d. lower neighboring tone   e. nota cambiata

4. a. 2–3 suspension   b. 4–3 suspension   c. 7–6 suspension

5. a. Dorian   b. Mixolydian   c. Aeolian

6. Errors are listed below:

1	Counterpoint must begin with second or fourth species—not third species.
1	Counterpoint above a cantus firmus must begin with an octave, a unison, or a 5th—not a 6th.
1–14	Too many quarter notes in a row.
9–11	Counterpoint outlines B–F dissonance.
10–11	Two dissonances in a row.
12–13	Parallel unisons.
14	Incorrect use of tie. First note should be a half note.
16	Accented neighboring tones not allowed.
19–20	Same note (B) should not be repeated.
20–22	Melodic movement by tritone (B to F) should be avoided.
21	Incorrect use of dissonance. Suspension implied but not resolved downward.
22–23	Parallel octaves.
23–24	Isolated pair of quarter notes.
25	Musica ficta required. C should be C♯.

Test Yourself 9

page 86

1. Errors are listed below:

1–2	Hidden (direct) octaves—soprano and bass.
3	Diminished triad in root position—should only be used in first inversion.
5–6	Parallel octaves and fifths.
9	No third factor.
12	No third factor.
12–13	Parallel octaves—tenor and soprano.
13	Doubled leading tone.

2.

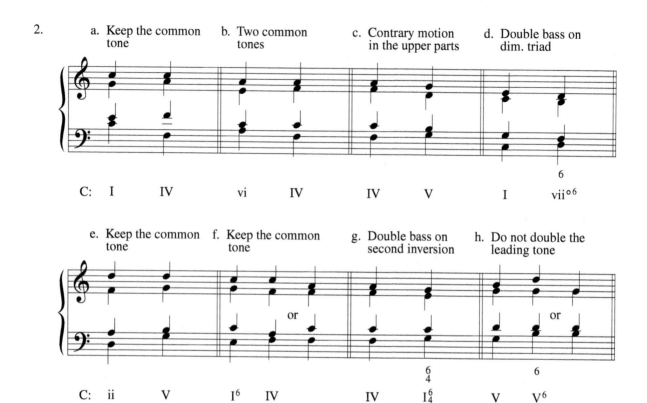

a. Keep the common tone   b. Two common tones   c. Contrary motion in the upper parts   d. Double bass on dim. triad

C: I   IV   vi   IV   IV   V   I   vii°⁶

e. Keep the common tone   f. Keep the common tone   g. Double bass on second inversion   h. Do not double the leading tone

or

or

C: ii   V   I⁶   IV   IV   I$^6_4$ V   V⁶

Test Yourself 10
page 99

1. a. 1, 5, 7, 8, 10, 12, 14, 15, 16
    b. (none)
    c. 2, 9
    d. 3, 4, 6, 11, 13

2. Circle progressions are more common than other progressions.

3. Circles indicate chord choices. Other answers are possible.

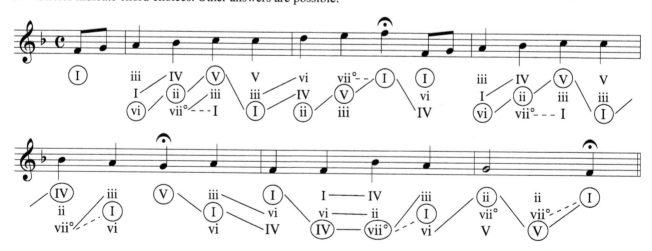

4. Bach's setting of the chorale is on page 172.

Test Yourself 11
page 113

1. a. G, bass, B
    b. B, alto, D
    c. D♭, alto, F
    d. B♭, alto, D♭
    e. A, soprano, C
    f. E♭, tenor, G

2. 3, 6, 9, and 11

3. 6

4. a. PT b. 4–3 SUS c. PT d. ANT e. PT f. P̃T

5. a. deceptive b. half c. imperfect authentic

Test Yourself 12
page 126

1. a. 1, 7, 8, 10, 13, 14, 20
    b. 3, 4, 17, 18
    c. 6, 12
    d. 9, 15, 16
    e. 2, 11
    f. 5, 19

2. a. Parallel 5ths (alto and tenor)
    b. 7th of the chord does not resolve downward by step
    c. Parallel 5ths (tenor and bass)

Test Yourself 13
page 135

1. a. No error
    b. Parallel 5ths (soprano and tenor)
    c. A2nd (alto)
    d. No error
    e. A2nd (alto), 7th of the chord does not resolve downward by step.
    f. 7th of the chord does not resolve downward by step.
    g. No error
    h. 7th of the chord does not resolve downward by step.
    i. No error

2. a. ii^7 V
    b. III^7 VI
    c. vi^7 ii
    d. iii^7 vi
    e. ii^{ø7} V
    f. I^7 IV

Test Yourself 14

1. a.

vii°⁶/V in the keys of D major and D minor
vii°⁶/ii in the key of G major
vii°⁶/iv in the key of E minor
vii°⁶/VI in the key of C♯ minor
vii°⁶/III in the key of F♯ minor

b.

V⁶₅/V in the keys of A♭ major and A♭ minor
V⁶₅/ii in the key of D♭ major
V⁶₅/iv in the key of B♭ minor
V⁶₅/vi in the key of G♭ major
V⁶₅/iii in the key of C♭ major

c.

V⁶/ii in the key of C major
V⁶/VI in the key of F♯ minor
V⁶/iii in the key of B♭ major
V⁶/V in the keys of G major and G minor
V⁶/IV in the key of A major

d.

vii°⁷/iv in the key of D minor
vii°⁷/iii in the key of E♭ major
vii°⁷/V in the keys of C major and C minor
vii°⁷/ii in the key of F major
vii°⁷/VI in the key of B minor

2.

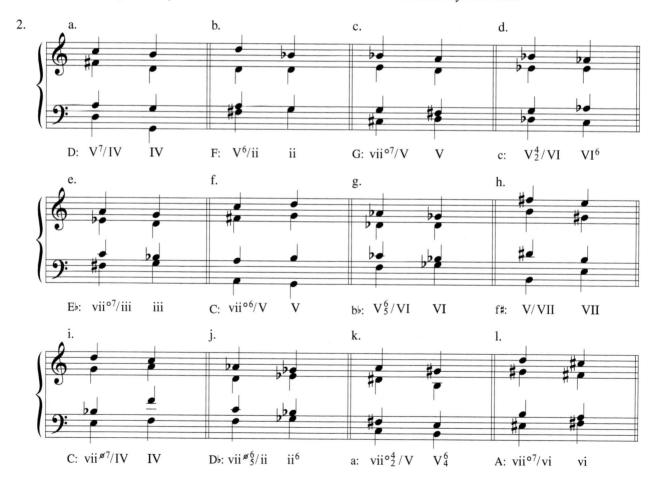

Test Yourself 15

page 161

1. b. | D: | I | ii | IV | vi |
   |---|---|---|---|---|
   | G: | IV | vi | I | iii |

   c. | f♯: | i | ii° | III | iv | v | VI | VII |
   |---|---|---|---|---|---|---|---|
   | A: | vi | vii° | I | ii | iii | IV | V |

   d. | e: | i | III | iv | VI |
   |---|---|---|---|---|
   | C: | iii | V | vi | I |

   e. | f: | i | III | iv | VI |
   |---|---|---|---|---|
   | D♭: | iii | V | vi | I |

   f. | B: | I | iii | V | vi |
   |---|---|---|---|---|
   | d♯: | VI | i | III | iv |

   g. | g♯: | i | ii° | iv | VI |
   |---|---|---|---|---|
   | B: | vi | vii° | ii | IV |

2.

C: I V^6 I   a: vi/i V^7 i

g: i VI V E♭: VI/I IV V^6 I

B♭: I vi ii^6 c: ii/i V^6 V i

d.

Ab: I   vi   V
c: i iii ii°⁶ i⁶₄ V i

e.

c: i i⁶ iv V
Eb: VI / IV vii°⁶ I

Test Yourself 16
page 164

1. The first section (measures 1–8) is open since it ends with a half cadence (away from the tonic chord). The second section (measures 9–18) is closed since it ends on the tonic.

2. The first section (measures 1–8) is open since it ends in the relative major (away from the *original* tonic chord). The second section (measures 9–34) is closed since it ends on the *original* tonic.

3. A *phrase* is a substantial musical thought usually ending with both a harmonic and melodic cadence. Two or more adjacent phrases may combine to form a *period.* An important characteristic of period construction is a relatively weaker cadence at the end of the first phrase (or phrases), and a strong cadence at the end of the final phrase. A *section* is a major division of a part form. Each section is a complete musical statement. By the definitions above, a *phrase* can never be a *period,* since a period must consist of two or more phrases. However, a *section* may (and often does) consist of a single *period,* so a period can be a section.

Test Yourself 17
page 166

1. The first section (measures 1–16) is closed, since it ends on the tonic chord (C major).

2. The second section (measures 17–32) is open, since it ends away from the original tonic chord (Ab major).

3. The B section acts as a contrasting section to the A section. It is often in a different key and has different melodic and rhythmic material. After the B section, the return to the A section is more pleasing, since it sounds "new" again.

4. In the *rounded binary form* the repetition of the first section (sometimes in part) occurs *within* the second section of the piece. It is not a separate section in itself. The rounded binary form retains its essential division into two parts.

5. The auxiliary members mentioned in the text are: introduction, transition, and coda.